I0020003

COMPUTER NETWORKING BOOTCAMP

ROUTING, SWITCHING AND TROUBLESHOOTING

4 BOOKS IN 1

BOOK 1
NETWORKING FUNDAMENTALS: A BEGINNER'S GUIDE TO ROUTING ESSENTIALS

BOOK 2
SWITCHING STRATEGIES: INTERMEDIATE TECHNIQUES FOR NETWORK OPTIMIZATION

BOOK 3
ADVANCED ROUTING PROTOCOLS: MASTERING COMPLEX NETWORK CONFIGURATIONS

BOOK 4
TROUBLESHOOTING MASTERY: EXPERT SOLUTIONS FOR RESOLVING NETWORK CHALLENGES

ROB BOTWRIGHT

Published by Rob Botwright
Library of Congress Cataloging-in-Publication Data
ISBN 978-1-83938-749-4
Cover design by Rizzo

Disclaimer

The contents of this book are based on extensive research and the best available historical sources. However, the author and publisher make no claims, promises, or guarantees about the accuracy, completeness, or adequacy of the information contained herein. The information in this book is provided on an "as is" basis, and the author and publisher disclaim any and all liability for any errors, omissions, or inaccuracies in the information or for any actions taken in reliance on such information. The opinions and views expressed in this book are those of the author and do not necessarily reflect the official policy or position of any organization or individual mentioned in this book. Any reference to specific people, places, or events is intended only to provide historical context and is not intended to defame or malign any group, individual, or entity. The information in this book is intended for educational and entertainment purposes only. It is not intended to be a substitute for professional advice or judgment. Readers are encouraged to conduct their own research and to seek professional advice where appropriate. Every effort has been made to obtain necessary permissions and acknowledgments for all images and other copyrighted material used in this book. Any errors or omissions in this regard are unintentional, and the author and publisher will correct them in future editions.

BOOK 1 - NETWORKING FUNDAMENTALS: A BEGINNER'S GUIDE TO ROUTING ESSENTIALS

Introduction 5
Chapter 1: Introduction to Computer Networking 8
Chapter 2: Understanding Network Topologies 14
Chapter 3: Overview of IP Addressing and Subnetting 20
Chapter 4: Basics of Routing Protocols 29
Chapter 5: Introduction to Cisco Networking Devices 36
Chapter 6: Configuring and Managing Network Switches 42
Chapter 7: Setting Up a Simple LAN (Local Area Network) 48
Chapter 8: Exploring Wireless Networking Concepts 56
Chapter 9: Network Security Fundamentals 63
Chapter 10: Troubleshooting Common Network Issues 71

BOOK 2 - SWITCHING STRATEGIES: INTERMEDIATE TECHNIQUES FOR NETWORK OPTIMIZATION

Chapter 1: Understanding VLANs (Virtual Local Area Networks) 80
Chapter 2: Implementing Spanning Tree Protocol (STP) 89
Chapter 3: Inter-VLAN Routing Techniques 97
Chapter 4: High Availability and Redundancy in Switching 104
Chapter 5: Quality of Service (QoS) in Switched Networks 112
Chapter 6: Port Security and Access Control Lists (ACLs) 120
Chapter 7: EtherChannel Configuration and Load Balancing 127
Chapter 8: Advanced Switching Technologies: VTP, PVST, and Rapid STP 134
Chapter 9: Multilayer Switching and Layer 3 Switching 141
Chapter 10: Virtual Switching System (VSS) Implementation and Management 150

BOOK 3 - ADVANCED ROUTING PROTOCOLS: MASTERING COMPLEX NETWORK CONFIGURATIONS

Chapter 1: Overview of Routing Protocols 158
Chapter 2: Advanced OSPF (Open Shortest Path First) Configuration 165
Chapter 3: EIGRP (Enhanced Interior Gateway Routing Protocol) Optimization 172
Chapter 4: BGP (Border Gateway Protocol) Essentials 180
Chapter 5: Route Redistribution Strategies 188
Chapter 6: Advanced Route Filtering Techniques 196
Chapter 7: Multicast Routing Protocols 202
Chapter 8: MPLS (Multiprotocol Label Switching) Fundamentals 208
Chapter 9: IPv6 Routing Considerations 214
Chapter 10: Network Scalability and Performance Optimization 221

BOOK 4 - TROUBLESHOOTING MASTERY: EXPERT SOLUTIONS FOR RESOLVING NETWORK CHALLENGES

Chapter 1: Understanding Network Troubleshooting Methodologies 229
Chapter 2: Analyzing Network Traffic with Packet Capture Tools 236
Chapter 3: Diagnosing Connectivity Issues: Layer 1 and Layer 2 Problems 243
Chapter 4: Addressing Common Layer 3 Routing Problems 249
Chapter 5: Troubleshooting WAN (Wide Area Network) Connectivity 256
Chapter 6: Dealing with Network Security Incidents and Threats 264
Chapter 7: Performance Tuning and Optimization Techniques 272
Chapter 8: Advanced Troubleshooting with Network Monitoring Tools 279
Chapter 9: Resolving VoIP (Voice over IP) and Video Conferencing Issues 286
Chapter 10: Disaster Recovery and Business Continuity Planning for Networks 293
Conclusion 300

Introduction

Welcome to the Computer Networking Bootcamp: Routing, Switching, and Troubleshooting bundle. In today's interconnected world, computer networking forms the backbone of modern communication and information exchange. Whether you are a novice looking to enter the field of networking or an experienced professional seeking to enhance your skills, this comprehensive bundle offers a structured approach to mastering the essentials of routing, switching, and troubleshooting.

Book 1, Networking Fundamentals: A Beginner's Guide to Routing Essentials, provides a solid foundation for understanding the core concepts of networking. From basic network architecture to routing essentials, this book equips beginners with the knowledge needed to navigate the complexities of modern networks.

Book 2, Switching Strategies: Intermediate Techniques for Network Optimization, builds upon the foundational knowledge acquired in the first book. Readers will explore advanced switching techniques such as VLANs, spanning tree protocols, and EtherChannel, enabling them to optimize network performance and scalability.

Book 3, Advanced Routing Protocols: Mastering Complex Network Configurations, delves into the intricacies of routing protocols such as OSPF, EIGRP, and BGP. Through detailed explanations and practical examples, readers will learn how to design, implement, and troubleshoot robust routing solutions for complex network configurations.

Book 4, Troubleshooting Mastery: Expert Solutions for Resolving Network Challenges, equips readers with the skills and techniques needed to diagnose and resolve a wide range of network issues effectively. With real-world scenarios and practical troubleshooting strategies, readers will learn how to identify problems, analyze symptoms, and implement solutions to keep networks running smoothly.

Whether you are looking to start a career in networking, advance your current skill set, or troubleshoot complex network challenges, the Computer Networking Bootcamp bundle offers invaluable insights and practical guidance to help you succeed in today's dynamic IT landscape. Get ready to embark on a journey of discovery and mastery as you explore the world of routing, switching, and troubleshooting.

BOOK 1
NETWORKING FUNDAMENTALS
A BEGINNER'S GUIDE TO ROUTING ESSENTIALS

ROB BOTWRIGHT

Chapter 1: Introduction to Computer Networking

Networking basics and concepts are essential knowledge for anyone venturing into the world of computer networking. At its core, networking is about connecting devices together to facilitate communication and resource sharing. Understanding the fundamental concepts lays the groundwork for building, managing, and troubleshooting networks effectively.

At the heart of networking is the concept of data transmission. Data travels across networks in the form of packets, which are small units of information. These packets contain both the data being transmitted and control information used by networking devices to route them to their destination.

One of the key components of any network is the network interface, which is the physical or logical connection point used by devices to communicate with each other. Network interfaces can take various forms, including Ethernet ports, wireless adapters, and virtual interfaces.

In addition to network interfaces, devices on a network are identified by unique addresses. In IPv4 networks, devices are assigned IP addresses, which are numerical identifiers used to differentiate them from other devices on the network. IPv6, the successor to IPv4, uses longer addresses to accommodate the growing number of connected devices.

To facilitate communication between devices on a network, networking protocols are used. These protocols define the rules and conventions for data exchange, ensuring that devices can understand and interpret the information being transmitted. Common networking protocols include TCP/IP, UDP, ICMP, and HTTP, each serving specific purposes within the network stack.

Networks can be classified based on their geographical scope. Local Area Networks (LANs) are confined to a single physical location, such as a home, office, or campus. LANs typically use Ethernet or Wi-Fi technology to connect devices within the same vicinity.

In contrast, Wide Area Networks (WANs) span larger geographical areas and may consist of multiple interconnected LANs. WANs often rely on leased lines, satellite links, or other long-distance communication technologies to connect distant locations.

To connect devices within a network and enable communication, networking devices such as routers, switches, and access points are used. Routers are responsible for forwarding data packets between different networks, while switches facilitate communication between devices within the same network. Access points provide wireless connectivity, allowing devices to connect to the network without physical cables.

In addition to wired and wireless networks, virtual networks have become increasingly prevalent in modern computing environments. Virtual networks use software-defined networking (SDN) technologies to create isolated network environments within a physical network infrastructure.

Security is a critical consideration in networking, given the potential risks associated with unauthorized access and data breaches. Various security measures, including firewalls, encryption, and access control lists (ACLs), are employed to protect networks from threats and vulnerabilities.

Network management is another vital aspect of networking, encompassing tasks such as network monitoring, configuration management, and performance optimization. Network administrators use specialized tools and techniques to ensure the smooth operation and reliability of network infrastructure.

In summary, networking basics and concepts provide the foundation for understanding how networks function and how to design, implement, and maintain them effectively. By mastering these fundamental principles, individuals can navigate the complexities of modern networking environments and contribute to the development of robust and secure networks.

The evolution of computer networking spans several decades, marked by significant advancements in technology and the proliferation of interconnected devices. It began in the early days of computing with isolated systems and has since transformed into a global network of interconnected devices, facilitating communication, collaboration, and resource sharing on an unprecedented scale.

The origins of computer networking can be traced back to the 1960s when early researchers sought ways to connect mainframe computers to enable remote access and resource sharing. One of the pioneering networking technologies of this era was ARPANET (Advanced Research Projects Agency Network), developed by the U.S. Department of Defense. ARPANET, which became operational in 1969, laid the groundwork for the modern internet by establishing the basic principles of packet switching and network protocols.

As computer networking continued to evolve, the 1970s saw the development of Ethernet, a widely used networking technology for local area networks (LANs). Ethernet enabled devices to communicate over a shared medium, typically using coaxial cables or twisted pair wiring. The adoption of Ethernet laid the foundation for the proliferation of LANs in businesses, educational institutions, and homes.

The 1980s witnessed the emergence of networking standards and protocols that would shape the future of computer networking. The Transmission Control Protocol/Internet Protocol (TCP/IP) emerged as the de facto standard for networking, providing a robust and scalable framework for communication between heterogeneous computer systems. TCP/IP, developed by researchers at DARPA (Defense Advanced Research Projects Agency), became the cornerstone of the internet and remains the dominant networking protocol to this day.

The 1990s saw the commercialization and popularization of the internet, fueled by advancements in networking hardware and software. The World Wide Web (WWW), invented by Tim Berners-Lee in 1989, revolutionized how information is accessed and shared on the internet. The widespread adoption of web browsers and the development of user-friendly interfaces made the internet accessible to a broader audience, leading to explosive growth in internet usage.

In parallel with the growth of the internet, the 1990s also saw the emergence of wireless networking technologies, such as Wi-Fi (IEEE 802.11). Wi-Fi enabled devices to connect to networks without the need for physical cables, ushering in an era of ubiquitous connectivity and mobile computing. Wi-Fi networks became commonplace in homes, offices, coffee shops, and other public spaces, providing users with seamless access to the internet and network resources.

The early 2000s witnessed the convergence of networking technologies, as voice, video, and data traffic began to traverse the same network infrastructure. This convergence gave rise to the concept of unified communications, where multiple modes of communication are integrated into a single platform. Voice over IP (VoIP) technology, which enables voice communication over IP networks, became increasingly popular as businesses sought to reduce costs and streamline communication.

The proliferation of mobile devices, such as smartphones and tablets, in the late 2000s and early 2010s further reshaped the landscape of computer networking. Mobile networking technologies, such as 3G, 4G, and now 5G, enable high-speed wireless connectivity on the go, empowering users to access the internet and cloud-based services from virtually anywhere.

The rise of cloud computing in the 2010s has further transformed the way networks are designed, deployed, and managed. Cloud computing enables organizations to offload their IT infrastructure to third-party providers, reducing costs and increasing scalability. This shift towards cloud-based services has led to the rise of software-defined networking (SDN), which allows for centralized management and programmable control of network infrastructure.

Looking ahead, the evolution of computer networking is poised to continue, driven by emerging technologies such as the Internet of Things (IoT), artificial intelligence (AI), and edge computing. These technologies promise to further expand the capabilities of networked devices and enable new applications and services that were previously unimaginable. As we embark on this journey of continued innovation and advancement, the evolution of computer networking will undoubtedly play a central role in shaping the future of technology and society.

Chapter 2: Understanding Network Topologies

Network topologies refer to the physical or logical layout of interconnected devices in a network, defining how data is transmitted between nodes. Understanding the various types of network topologies is crucial for designing, deploying, and managing efficient and reliable networks.

One of the most common network topologies is the bus topology, where all devices are connected to a single communication line, called a bus. In a bus topology, data travels along the bus and is received by all devices connected to it. To deploy a bus topology, devices are connected to the bus using coaxial cables or twisted pair cables, with terminators placed at both ends of the bus to prevent signal reflections.

Another widely used network topology is the star topology, where each device is connected to a central hub or switch. In a star topology, data travels from one device to the central hub, which then forwards it to the intended recipient. This type of topology offers advantages such as ease of installation, scalability, and fault tolerance, as a single device failure does not affect the rest of the network.

A variation of the star topology is the extended star topology, which includes multiple interconnected hubs or switches. In an extended star topology, devices are connected to local hubs, which are then connected to a central hub or switch. This architecture allows for greater scalability and flexibility in network design, as additional hubs can be added to accommodate more devices.

The ring topology is another type of network topology where devices are connected in a closed loop configuration. In a ring topology, data travels in one direction around the ring, with each device acting as a repeater to regenerate the signal. While ring topologies offer advantages such as simplicity and fault tolerance, a single device failure can disrupt the entire network unless proper redundancy measures are in place.

Mesh topologies are characterized by multiple interconnected devices, where each device has a direct connection to every other device in the network. Mesh topologies can be either full mesh, where every device is connected to every other device, or partial mesh, where only certain devices have direct connections. Mesh topologies offer high redundancy and fault tolerance, as data can be rerouted through alternate paths in the event of a link failure.

Hybrid topologies combine two or more types of network topologies to create a customized network architecture that meets specific requirements. For example, a hybrid topology may combine elements of a star topology with elements of a mesh topology to achieve both centralized control and high redundancy. Hybrid topologies offer flexibility and scalability, allowing organizations to design networks that balance performance, reliability, and cost.

The choice of network topology depends on various factors, including the size and layout of the network, the number of devices, bandwidth requirements, and fault tolerance considerations. Before deploying a network topology, it is essential to carefully assess these factors and choose the topology that best meets the organization's needs.

In addition to physical network topologies, logical network topologies define how data is transmitted between devices at the protocol level. Common logical topologies include Ethernet, Token Ring, and ATM (Asynchronous Transfer Mode), each of which uses different protocols and techniques for data transmission.

In summary, understanding the different types of network topologies is essential for designing, deploying, and managing efficient and reliable networks. Whether deploying a simple bus topology or a complex hybrid topology, careful consideration of network requirements and topology characteristics is crucial for building a network that meets the needs of the organization.

Network topologies play a crucial role in determining the efficiency, scalability, and fault tolerance of a network, each offering distinct advantages and disadvantages. Understanding these pros and cons is essential for selecting the most appropriate topology for a given networking environment.

One of the most common network topologies is the bus topology, characterized by simplicity and cost-effectiveness. In a bus topology, all devices are connected to a single communication line, making it easy to set up and maintain. However, bus topologies are susceptible to single points of failure, as a break in the bus cable can disrupt communication for all devices connected to it. Moreover, bus topologies suffer from limited scalability, as adding more devices can degrade performance due to increased collisions on the shared medium.

A star topology addresses many of the limitations of a bus topology by centralizing connectivity through a central hub or switch. This topology offers better fault tolerance, as a single device failure does not affect the rest of the network. Additionally, star topologies support greater scalability, as additional devices can be easily added to the network without impacting existing devices. However, star topologies are more expensive to deploy compared to bus topologies due to the need for a central hub or switch. Moreover, the central hub represents a single point of failure, and if it malfunctions, the entire network may become inaccessible.

A ring topology, where devices are connected in a closed loop configuration, offers simplicity and fault tolerance. In a ring topology, data travels in one direction around the ring, with each device acting as a repeater to regenerate the signal. This topology eliminates the need for a central hub or switch, reducing costs and points of failure. However, ring topologies suffer from limited scalability, as adding more devices can introduce latency and increase the risk of collisions. Additionally, a single device failure can disrupt the entire network unless proper redundancy measures, such as dual ring configurations, are in place.

Mesh topologies offer the highest level of fault tolerance and redundancy by providing multiple interconnected paths between devices. In a full mesh topology, every device is connected to every other device, ensuring that data can be rerouted through alternate paths in the event of a link failure. This topology offers excellent fault tolerance and scalability, but it is also the most expensive to deploy and maintain due to the high number of interconnections required. Partial mesh topologies offer a compromise between fault tolerance and cost by selectively connecting certain devices to multiple others.

Hybrid topologies combine two or more types of network topologies to create a customized network architecture that meets specific requirements. For example, a hybrid topology may combine elements of a star topology with elements of a mesh topology to achieve both centralized control and high redundancy. Hybrid topologies offer flexibility and scalability, allowing organizations to design networks that balance performance, reliability, and cost. However, hybrid topologies can be complex to design and deploy, requiring careful planning to ensure compatibility and interoperability between different topology types.

In addition to physical network topologies, logical network topologies define how data is transmitted between devices at the protocol level. Common logical topologies include Ethernet, Token Ring, and ATM (Asynchronous Transfer Mode), each of which uses different protocols and techniques for data transmission.

In summary, the choice of network topology depends on various factors, including the size and layout of the network, bandwidth requirements, fault tolerance considerations, and budget constraints. By carefully evaluating the advantages and disadvantages of different topologies, organizations can design and deploy networks that meet their specific needs and requirements.

Chapter 3: Overview of IP Addressing and Subnetting

IPv4 addressing is a fundamental aspect of computer networking, providing a unique numerical identifier to each device connected to a network, enabling communication and data transfer between them. In IPv4, addresses are 32 bits long and are typically represented in dotted-decimal notation, consisting of four octets separated by periods. Each octet represents a byte of the address, with values ranging from 0 to 255. For example, an IPv4 address might be expressed as 192.168.1.1.

IPv4 addresses are divided into different classes, each serving a specific purpose and addressing range. The five classes of IPv4 addresses are Class A, Class B, Class C, Class D, and Class E.

Class A addresses are used for large networks and have their first bit set to 0. The first octet represents the network portion of the address, and the remaining three octets represent the host portion. Class A addresses range from 1.0.0.0 to 126.0.0.0, with 127.0.0.0 reserved for loopback testing.

Class B addresses are used for medium-sized networks and have their first two bits set to 10. The first two octets represent the network portion of the address, and the remaining two octets represent the host portion. Class B addresses range from 128.0.0.0 to 191.255.0.0.

Class C addresses are used for small networks and have their first three bits set to 110. The first three octets represent the network portion of the address, and the last octet represents the host portion. Class C addresses range from 192.0.0.0 to 223.255.255.0.

Class D addresses are reserved for multicast communication and have their first four bits set to 1110. These addresses range from 224.0.0.0 to 239.255.255.255 and are used for one-to-many communication, where a single packet is sent to multiple recipients.

Class E addresses are reserved for experimental use and have their first four bits set to 1111. These addresses range from 240.0.0.0 to 255.255.255.255 and are not typically used in practice.

In addition to the address class, IPv4 addresses are further subdivided into network and host portions. The subnet mask is used to determine which bits of an IPv4 address represent the network portion and which bits represent the host portion. Subnet masks are also represented in dotted-decimal notation, with 1s indicating the network portion and 0s indicating the host portion. For example, a subnet mask of 255.255.255.0 indicates that the first 24 bits of the IPv4 address represent the network portion, and the last 8 bits represent the host portion.

IPv4 addresses can be assigned statically or dynamically, depending on the network configuration. Static IP addressing involves manually assigning an IP address to a device, typically through configuration settings on the device itself or through a DHCP (Dynamic Host Configuration Protocol) server. To assign a static IPv4 address to a device using the command line interface (CLI), the following steps can be followed:

Access the device's CLI interface.

Enter the configuration mode, if applicable, using a command such as **configure terminal**.

Navigate to the interface configuration mode for the desired interface using a command such as **interface <interface name>**.

Assign the static IPv4 address to the interface using the **ip address <ip address> <subnet mask>** command.

Optionally, configure additional parameters such as the default gateway and DNS server settings.

Dynamic IP addressing, on the other hand, involves automatically assigning IP addresses to devices using a DHCP server. DHCP servers lease IP addresses to devices on the network for a predetermined period, eliminating the need for manual IP address configuration. To configure a device to obtain an IPv4 address dynamically using DHCP, the following steps can be followed:

Access the device's CLI interface.

Enter the configuration mode, if applicable, using a command such as **configure terminal**.

Navigate to the interface configuration mode for the desired interface using a command such as **interface <interface name>**.

Enable DHCP on the interface using the **ip address dhcp** command.

Optionally, configure additional DHCP parameters such as DHCP relay settings and DHCP server address.

IPv4 addresses are also subject to subnetting, a technique used to divide a single network into smaller, more manageable subnetworks. Subnetting allows for efficient use of IP address space and helps minimize network congestion by reducing the number of devices in each broadcast domain. To subnet an IPv4 network, the following steps can be followed:

Determine the desired number of subnets and hosts per subnet.

Choose an appropriate subnet mask based on the number of required subnets and hosts per subnet.

Apply the chosen subnet mask to the IPv4 address space to divide it into subnets.

Assign subnet addresses to each subnet and allocate host addresses within each subnet.

In summary, IPv4 addressing is a critical component of computer networking, providing a unique numerical identifier to each device connected to a network. By understanding the different classes of IPv4 addresses, subnetting techniques, and IP address assignment methods, network administrators can design and deploy efficient and reliable networks that meet the needs of their organizations.

Subnetting is a fundamental concept in computer networking that involves dividing a single, larger network into smaller, more manageable subnetworks. This technique allows for efficient use of IP address space and helps minimize network congestion by reducing the number of devices in each broadcast domain. Subnetting is essential for optimizing network performance and scalability, particularly in large enterprise environments where numerous devices need to be interconnected.

To understand subnetting fundamentals, it's crucial to grasp the concept of IP addresses and subnet masks. IP addresses are unique numerical identifiers assigned to devices connected to a network, enabling communication and data transfer between them. Subnet masks, on the other hand, determine which portion of an IP address represents the network portion and which portion represents the host portion. Subnet masks are represented in dotted-decimal notation, with 1s indicating the network portion and 0s indicating the host portion.

One of the key benefits of subnetting is the ability to create smaller, more manageable broadcast domains within a larger network. Broadcast domains are segments of a network where broadcast packets are forwarded, and devices within the same broadcast domain can communicate with each other directly. By dividing a network into smaller subnets, the number of devices in each broadcast domain is reduced, which helps minimize network congestion and improves overall network performance.

Subnetting also enables organizations to optimize IP address allocation and conserve address space. In many cases, organizations are assigned a block of IP addresses, known as a subnet, by their Internet Service Provider (ISP). By subnetting this block of addresses into smaller subnets, organizations can allocate IP addresses more efficiently, ensuring that each subnet has sufficient addresses for its specific requirements.

One of the most common methods used to subnet a network is Variable Length Subnet Masking (VLSM). VLSM allows for the creation of subnets with varying sizes, depending on the number of hosts required in each subnet. This flexibility enables network administrators to tailor subnets to specific requirements, allocating more IP addresses to larger subnets and fewer IP addresses to smaller subnets.

To subnet a network using VLSM, network administrators must first determine the number of subnets and hosts required for each subnet. Once these requirements are known, the network can be subnetted accordingly using a subnet calculator or by performing manual calculations. For example, to subnet a Class C network address (e.g., 192.168.1.0) into multiple subnets with varying sizes, the following steps can be followed:

Determine the number of subnets required based on the organization's network topology and growth projections.

Determine the number of hosts required for each subnet, taking into account factors such as the number of devices, servers, and network infrastructure components.

Calculate the subnet mask for each subnet based on the number of required subnets and hosts per subnet. Subnet masks are typically represented in CIDR (Classless Inter-Domain Routing) notation, which specifies the number of bits used for the network portion of the address (e.g., /24).

Apply the subnet masks to the network address to create the desired subnets. This can be done by bitwise ANDing the subnet mask with the network address to obtain the subnet addresses.

Allocate IP addresses to devices within each subnet, ensuring that each device has a unique IP address within its respective subnet.

By following these steps, network administrators can subnet a network using VLSM to create smaller, more manageable subnets that meet the organization's specific requirements.

Another subnetting technique commonly used in computer networking is Classless Inter-Domain Routing (CIDR). CIDR allows for more efficient use of IP address space by allowing networks to be allocated non-contiguous blocks of addresses. With CIDR, network addresses are represented in the form of a prefix followed by a slash and a number, indicating the number of bits used for the network portion of the address (e.g., 192.168.1.0/24).

CIDR notation simplifies subnetting and IP address allocation by providing a concise way to represent network addresses and subnet masks. For example, a network address of 192.168.1.0 with a subnet mask of 255.255.255.0 can be represented as 192.168.1.0/24 in CIDR notation. This notation indicates that the first 24 bits of the address represent the network portion, while the remaining 8 bits represent the host portion.

To subnet a network using CIDR notation, network administrators must first determine the desired subnet size and the number of subnets required. Once these requirements are known, the network can be subnetted accordingly using CIDR notation to represent the subnet masks. For example, to subnet a Class B network address (e.g., 172.16.0.0) into multiple subnets with varying sizes, the following steps can be followed:

Determine the number of subnets required based on the organization's network topology and growth projections.

Determine the desired subnet size, expressed as a CIDR prefix length (e.g., /26 for a subnet with 64 hosts).

Apply CIDR notation to represent the subnet masks for each subnet. For example, a /26 subnet mask would be represented as 255.255.255.192 or 172.16.0.0/26.

Allocate IP addresses to devices within each subnet, ensuring that each device has a unique IP address within its respective subnet.

By subnetting a network using CIDR notation, network administrators can create smaller, more efficient subnets that meet the organization's specific requirements while conserving IP address space.

In summary, subnetting is a fundamental concept in computer networking that involves dividing a single, larger network into smaller, more manageable subnetworks. By subnetting a network, organizations can optimize IP address allocation, improve network performance, and enhance scalability. Whether using techniques such as VLSM or CIDR, subnetting enables network administrators to create efficient and reliable networks that meet the needs of their organizations.

Chapter 4: Basics of Routing Protocols

Distance Vector Routing is a classic routing algorithm used in computer networking to determine the best path for data packets to travel from a source to a destination across an internetwork. This routing algorithm is based on the principle of sharing routing information between neighboring routers, which then use this information to make forwarding decisions. In a Distance Vector Routing algorithm, each router maintains a routing table that contains information about the distance (cost) to reach each destination network and the next-hop router to reach that destination. The distance is typically measured in terms of hops, where each hop represents a network segment traversed by the data packet.

One of the most commonly used Distance Vector Routing protocols is the Routing Information Protocol (RIP). RIP operates by periodically broadcasting routing updates to neighboring routers, informing them of the current state of the network. Each router then updates its routing table based on these updates, selecting the best path to each destination based on the shortest hop count. RIP uses a maximum hop count of 15 to prevent routing loops and to ensure network convergence. When a router receives a routing update with a hop count greater than 15, it considers the destination unreachable.

To deploy Distance Vector Routing using RIP, network administrators must configure RIP on each router in the network. This can be done using the following commands in the router's CLI interface:

cssCopy code

router rip network <network address>

The "router rip" command enters the RIP configuration mode, allowing administrators to configure RIP-specific parameters. The "network <network address>" command specifies which networks are participating in RIP routing. This command tells the router to advertise routing information for the specified network to neighboring routers.

Once RIP is configured on all routers in the network, each router will begin exchanging routing updates with its neighbors, sharing information about the reachable destinations and the associated hop counts. These updates are exchanged using RIP's routing update mechanism, which uses User Datagram Protocol (UDP) packets sent to port 520.

While Distance Vector Routing algorithms like RIP are simple and easy to implement, they suffer from certain limitations, particularly in large networks with complex topologies. One of the main drawbacks of Distance Vector Routing is the slow convergence time, which refers to the time it takes for the network to reach a stable state after a topology change. Due to its periodic update mechanism and the limited information shared between routers, Distance Vector

Routing algorithms may take a significant amount of time to converge, leading to potential network instability and suboptimal routing decisions.

Another limitation of Distance Vector Routing is its susceptibility to routing loops and count-to-infinity problems. Routing loops occur when routers inadvertently forward packets in a circular path due to incorrect routing information. Count-to-infinity problems occur when routers incorrectly report longer paths to a destination as shorter paths, leading to routing loops. To mitigate these issues, Distance Vector Routing protocols like RIP employ various mechanisms such as split horizon, poison reverse, and hold-down timers to prevent routing loops and ensure network stability.

Despite its limitations, Distance Vector Routing remains a widely used routing algorithm in small to medium-sized networks due to its simplicity and ease of implementation. However, in larger and more complex networks, where fast convergence and scalability are critical, more advanced routing protocols such as Link State Routing or Enhanced Interior Gateway Routing Protocol (EIGRP) may be preferred.

Overall, Distance Vector Routing provides a basic yet effective mechanism for routing data packets in computer networks, allowing routers to make forwarding decisions based on distance information obtained from neighboring routers. By understanding the principles and characteristics of Distance Vector

Routing, network administrators can design and deploy efficient and reliable networks that meet the needs of their organizations.

Link State Routing is a sophisticated routing algorithm used in computer networking to determine the best path for data packets to travel from a source to a destination across an internetwork. Unlike Distance Vector Routing, which relies on periodic updates and hop count to make routing decisions, Link State Routing is based on the concept of flooding link state information throughout the network to build a complete and accurate map of the network topology. This approach enables routers to calculate the shortest path to each destination using algorithms such as Dijkstra's shortest path algorithm.

One of the most widely used Link State Routing protocols is the Open Shortest Path First (OSPF) protocol. OSPF operates by routers exchanging link state advertisements (LSAs) with their neighboring routers, which contain information about the router's directly connected links and the state of those links. Each router then uses this information to build a link state database, which represents a comprehensive view of the network topology. By applying Dijkstra's shortest path algorithm to the link state database, routers can calculate the shortest path to each destination and populate their routing tables accordingly.

To deploy OSPF on a network, network administrators must configure OSPF on each router and specify which networks are participating in OSPF routing. This can be done using the following commands in the router's CLI interface:

phpCopy code

```
router ospf <process ID> network <network address> <wildcard mask> area <area ID>
```

The "router ospf <process ID>" command enters the OSPF configuration mode, allowing administrators to configure OSPF-specific parameters. The "network <network address> <wildcard mask> area <area ID>" command specifies which networks are participating in OSPF routing and assigns them to a specific OSPF area. OSPF areas are used to partition large OSPF networks into smaller, more manageable segments, which helps reduce routing overhead and improves network scalability.

Once OSPF is configured on all routers in the network, each router will begin exchanging link state advertisements with its neighboring routers, flooding the LSAs throughout the network to build a complete and accurate view of the network topology. Routers then use this information to calculate the shortest path to each destination and populate their routing tables accordingly.

One of the key advantages of Link State Routing protocols like OSPF is their fast convergence time. Unlike Distance Vector Routing protocols, which rely on periodic updates and hop count to converge, Link

State Routing protocols converge quickly in response to network topology changes. This is because routers only need to flood changes in link state information to their neighboring routers, rather than waiting for periodic updates to propagate through the network.

Another advantage of Link State Routing protocols is their scalability and efficiency in large networks. By dividing the network into smaller OSPF areas and summarizing routes between areas, OSPF reduces routing overhead and improves network scalability. Additionally, Link State Routing protocols support features such as authentication, route summarization, and policy-based routing, which provide greater flexibility and control over routing decisions.

Despite its advantages, Link State Routing protocols like OSPF also have certain limitations. One limitation is the complexity of OSPF configuration and maintenance, particularly in large and complex networks. OSPF requires careful planning and design to ensure proper area placement, route summarization, and convergence optimization. Additionally, OSPF consumes more router resources and bandwidth compared to Distance Vector Routing protocols, due to the need to flood LSAs throughout the network.

Another limitation of Link State Routing protocols is their susceptibility to network instability caused by LSAs flooding. If a router generates an excessive number of LSAs or if LSAs are flooded too frequently, it can lead to network congestion and instability. To mitigate this risk, network administrators must carefully tune OSPF parameters such as hello and dead intervals, LSA throttling, and flooding reduction techniques.

Overall, Link State Routing protocols like OSPF provide a robust and efficient mechanism for routing data packets in computer networks, enabling routers to make optimal routing decisions based on complete and accurate information about the network topology. By understanding the principles and characteristics of Link State Routing, network administrators can design and deploy efficient and reliable networks that meet the needs of their organizations.

Chapter 5: Introduction to Cisco Networking Devices

Cisco offers a wide range of router models designed to meet the diverse networking needs of organizations of all sizes and industries. These routers vary in terms of performance, features, scalability, and price, allowing organizations to choose the model that best fits their specific requirements. Cisco router models are categorized into several series, each targeting different market segments and use cases.

One of the most popular series of Cisco router models is the Cisco 800 series, which is designed for small office and home office (SOHO) environments. The Cisco 800 series routers are compact, cost-effective, and easy to deploy, making them ideal for small businesses and remote branch offices. These routers typically support basic routing, security, and wireless capabilities, providing essential connectivity for small-scale networks. CLI commands for configuring basic settings on a Cisco 800 series router include:

csharpCopy code

```
enable configure terminal hostname <hostname>
interface <interface> ip address <ip address>
<subnet mask> no shutdown exit
```

Another series of Cisco router models is the Cisco ISR (Integrated Services Router) series, which is designed for medium to large enterprise environments. The Cisco ISR series routers offer a wide range of features and capabilities, including advanced routing, security, voice, and wireless services. These routers are highly modular and scalable, allowing organizations to customize their configurations to meet specific requirements. CLI commands for configuring advanced features on a Cisco ISR series router include:

phpCopy code

```
enable configure terminal router ospf <process ID> network <network address> <wildcard mask> area <area ID> exit ip route <destination network> <subnet mask> <next-hop address> exit
```

The Cisco ASR (Aggregation Services Router) series is another series of high-performance routers designed for large-scale enterprise and service provider networks. The Cisco ASR series routers offer industry-leading performance, scalability, and reliability, making them ideal for mission-critical applications and high-demand environments. These routers support advanced features such as high-speed WAN connectivity, traffic management, and service virtualization. CLI commands for configuring advanced features on a Cisco ASR series router include:

csharpCopy code

```
enable configure terminal interface <interface> bandwidth <bandwidth> ip address <ip address> <subnet mask> no shutdown exit
```

The Cisco Catalyst series routers are designed for data center and campus networking environments, offering high-density, high-performance switching capabilities. These routers support advanced features such as VLANs, QoS, and multicast routing, making them ideal for converged networking deployments. CLI commands for configuring VLANs on a Cisco Catalyst series router include:

phpCopy code

enable configure terminal vlan <vlan ID> name <vlan name> exit interface <interface> switchport mode access switchport access vlan <vlan ID> exit

In addition to these series, Cisco offers specialized router models for specific use cases and industries. For example, the Cisco RV series routers are designed for small businesses and remote offices, offering built-in security features and easy-to-use management interfaces. The Cisco Cloud Services Router (CSR) series routers are virtualized routers designed for cloud-based networking environments, offering the flexibility and scalability of software-defined networking (SDN).

Overall, Cisco router models are designed to provide organizations with reliable, scalable, and secure networking solutions to meet their evolving business needs. Whether deploying routers in small office environments or large-scale enterprise networks, Cisco offers a diverse portfolio of router models to suit every requirement. By understanding the capabilities and features of Cisco router models, organizations can make informed decisions about their networking infrastructure and ensure seamless connectivity for their users and applications.

Cisco offers a comprehensive range of switch models designed to meet the diverse networking needs of organizations across various industries and scales. These switches vary in terms of performance, features, scalability, and price, enabling organizations to select the most suitable model based on their specific requirements. Cisco switch models are categorized into different series, each targeting specific market segments and use cases.

One of the most widely deployed series of Cisco switch models is the Cisco Catalyst series, which is designed for campus and data center networking environments. The Catalyst series switches offer a wide range of features and capabilities, including high-speed Ethernet connectivity, advanced Layer 2 and Layer 3 switching, and comprehensive security and management features. These switches are available in various form factors, including fixed-configuration and modular switches, to accommodate different deployment scenarios.

CLI commands for configuring basic settings on a Cisco Catalyst switch include:

csharpCopy code

```
enable configure terminal hostname <hostname>
interface <interface> switchport mode access
switchport access vlan <vlan ID> no shutdown exit
```

Another popular series of Cisco switch models is the Cisco Nexus series, which is designed for data center networking and high-performance computing environments. The Nexus series switches offer ultra-low-latency switching, high-density 10/40/100 Gigabit Ethernet (GbE) connectivity, and advanced features such as virtualization, fabric extensibility, and software-defined networking (SDN) support. These switches are ideal for demanding applications such as cloud computing, big data analytics, and high-frequency trading.

CLI commands for configuring VLANs on a Cisco Nexus switch include:

phpCopy code

```
configure terminal vlan <vlan ID> name <vlan name>
exit interface <interface> switchport mode access
switchport access vlan <vlan ID> exit
```

The Cisco Meraki series switches are another series of Cisco switch models designed for cloud-managed networking environments. These switches offer simple deployment, centralized management, and advanced features such as Layer 7 application visibility and control, automatic traffic optimization, and integrated security features. The Meraki series switches are ideal for small to medium-sized businesses and distributed branch offices that require easy-to-manage and scalable networking solutions.

CLI commands for configuring basic settings on a Cisco Meraki switch are not applicable, as these switches are managed through the Cisco Meraki dashboard, a cloud-based management platform.

The Cisco Small Business series switches are designed for small businesses and remote branch offices, offering cost-effective and easy-to-deploy switching solutions. These switches provide basic Layer 2 switching capabilities, simple management interfaces, and support for essential networking features such as VLANs, Quality of Service (QoS), and link aggregation. The Small Business series switches are ideal for organizations with limited IT resources and budget constraints.

CLI commands for configuring VLANs on a Cisco Small Business switch include:

phpCopy code

enable configure terminal vlan database vlan <vlan ID> name <vlan name> exit interface <interface> switchport mode access switchport access vlan <vlan ID> exit

In addition to these series, Cisco offers specialized switch models for specific use cases and industries. For example, the Cisco Industrial Ethernet series switches are designed for harsh industrial environments, offering ruggedized designs, wide temperature ranges, and support for industrial protocols such as PROFINET and Modbus. These switches are ideal for applications such as factory automation, transportation, and energy production.

Overall, Cisco switch models provide organizations with reliable, scalable, and feature-rich networking solutions to meet their evolving business needs. Whether deploying switches in campus networks, data centers, small businesses, or industrial environments, Cisco offers a diverse portfolio of switch models to suit every requirement. By understanding the capabilities and features of Cisco switch models, organizations can make informed decisions about their networking infrastructure and ensure seamless connectivity for their users and applications.

Chapter 6: Configuring and Managing Network Switches

VLAN configuration is a fundamental aspect of network design, allowing network administrators to segment a single physical network into multiple logical networks, or VLANs, thereby improving network efficiency, security, and manageability. VLANs enable devices within the same VLAN to communicate with each other as if they were on the same physical network, while devices in different VLANs are isolated from each other. VLAN configuration involves several steps, including creating VLANs, assigning VLAN membership to switch ports, and configuring inter-VLAN routing where necessary.

The first step in VLAN configuration is to create the VLANs themselves on the network switches. This can be done using the following CLI command on a Cisco switch:

phpCopy code

```
configure terminal vlan <vlan ID> name <vlan name>
exit
```

In this command, "vlan <vlan ID>" creates a new VLAN with the specified VLAN ID, and "name <vlan name>" assigns a name to the VLAN for easier identification. Once the VLANs are created, the next step is to assign VLAN membership to switch ports. This is done by configuring the switch ports to be access ports and assigning them to the desired VLAN. The following CLI command accomplishes this:

csharpCopy code

interface <interface> switchport mode access switchport access vlan <vlan ID>

In this command, "interface <interface>" specifies the switch port to be configured, "switchport mode access" sets the port to be an access port, and "switchport access vlan <vlan ID>" assigns the port to the specified VLAN. Repeat these commands for each switch port that needs to be assigned to a VLAN.

In addition to access ports, VLAN configuration may also involve configuring trunk ports, which are used to carry traffic for multiple VLANs across a single physical link. Trunk ports are typically used to interconnect switches or to connect switches to routers or other networking devices. The following CLI command configures a switch port as a trunk port:

csharpCopy code

interface <interface> switchport mode trunk

This command sets the specified switch port to operate in trunk mode, allowing it to carry traffic for multiple VLANs. By default, all VLANs are allowed to traverse the trunk port, but VLAN pruning can be used to restrict the VLANs that are allowed to traverse the trunk. VLAN pruning helps reduce unnecessary traffic on the trunk link and improve network performance.

In some cases, VLANs may need to communicate with each other, which requires inter-VLAN routing. Inter-VLAN routing allows traffic to flow between VLANs by routing it through a router or Layer 3 switch. To configure inter-VLAN routing on a router, the following CLI commands can be used:

csharpCopy code

```
interface <interface> ip address <ip address> <subnet mask> no shutdown
```

In these commands, "interface <interface>" specifies the router interface connected to the VLANs, "ip address <ip address> <subnet mask>" assigns an IP address and subnet mask to the interface, and "no shutdown" enables the interface. Once the router interfaces are configured, routing protocols or static routes can be used to enable communication between VLANs.

In summary, VLAN configuration is an essential aspect of network design, allowing network administrators to segment networks for improved efficiency, security, and manageability. By following the steps outlined above and using CLI commands to create VLANs, assign VLAN membership to switch ports, configure trunk ports, and enable inter-VLAN routing where necessary, administrators can effectively configure VLANs to meet the specific requirements of their networks.

Switch port security is a crucial aspect of network security that involves implementing measures to control access to switch ports and prevent unauthorized devices from connecting to the network. By securing switch ports, organizations can mitigate the risk of unauthorized access, data breaches, and network attacks. Switch port security can be implemented using various techniques and features, including MAC address filtering, port security, and 802.1X authentication.

One of the most common techniques used to secure switch ports is MAC address filtering, which allows network administrators to specify which devices are allowed to connect to specific switch ports based on their MAC addresses. This technique is implemented using the following CLI command on a Cisco switch:

csharpCopy code

```
interface <interface> switchport port-security
switchport port-security mac-address <mac address>
```

In this command, "interface <interface>" specifies the switch port to be configured for port security, "switchport port-security" enables port security on the interface, and "switchport port-security mac-address <mac address>" specifies the MAC address of the authorized device. Multiple MAC addresses can be configured for each switch port, allowing multiple devices to connect to the port.

Another common technique used for switch port security is port security, which limits the number of MAC addresses allowed to connect to a switch port and takes action if the limit is exceeded. This technique is particularly useful in environments where the number of devices connected to each switch port is known and limited. Port security can be configured using the following CLI command:

csharpCopy code

interface <interface> switchport port-security maximum <max addresses>

In this command, "interface <interface>" specifies the switch port to be configured for port security, and "switchport port-security maximum <max addresses>" sets the maximum number of MAC addresses allowed to connect to the port. If the number of MAC addresses exceeds the configured limit, the port can be configured to take specific actions, such as shutting down the port or sending an alert to the network administrator.

802.1X authentication is another effective technique used for switch port security, which requires devices to authenticate themselves before being allowed to connect to the network. This technique is commonly used in enterprise environments to ensure that only authorized devices can access the network. 802.1X authentication involves three main components: the supplicant (the client device), the authenticator (the switch port), and the authentication server (such as a RADIUS server). The following CLI command can be used to configure 802.1X authentication on a switch port:

vbnetCopy code

interface <interface> dot1x port-control {force-authorized | force-unauthorized | auto}

In this command, "interface <interface>" specifies the switch port to be configured for 802.1X authentication, and "dot1x port-control {force-authorized | force-unauthorized | auto}" configures the port to control the behavior of unauthenticated devices. The "force-authorized" option allows all devices to connect to the port regardless of authentication status, "force-

46

unauthorized" blocks all devices from connecting until they are authenticated, and "auto" enables 802.1X authentication and allows devices to connect if they successfully authenticate.

In addition to these techniques, switch port security can also be enhanced by implementing additional features such as DHCP snooping, dynamic ARP inspection (DAI), and IP source guard. DHCP snooping prevents rogue DHCP servers from distributing invalid IP addresses, while DAI validates ARP packets to prevent ARP spoofing attacks. IP source guard filters IP traffic based on the source IP address, preventing IP address spoofing attacks.

Overall, switch port security is an essential component of network security that helps protect against unauthorized access, data breaches, and network attacks. By implementing techniques such as MAC address filtering, port security, and 802.1X authentication, organizations can effectively control access to switch ports and safeguard their network infrastructure. By using CLI commands to configure switch port security features, network administrators can ensure that their networks remain secure and resilient against evolving threats.

Chapter 7: Setting Up a Simple LAN (Local Area Network)

LAN design considerations are crucial for creating efficient, scalable, and resilient local area networks that meet the needs of modern organizations. LAN design involves various aspects, including network topology, network segmentation, addressing schemes, cabling infrastructure, and network equipment selection. By carefully considering these factors, network architects can design LANs that provide high performance, reliability, and security for users and applications.

One of the key considerations in LAN design is selecting the appropriate network topology. The network topology defines the physical and logical layout of the network, including how devices are interconnected. Common network topologies include star, bus, ring, and mesh. Each topology has its advantages and disadvantages in terms of scalability, fault tolerance, and ease of management. For example, a star topology, where all devices are connected to a central switch or hub, provides centralized management and fault isolation but may suffer from single points of failure. On the other hand, a mesh topology, where every device is connected to every other device, offers high redundancy and fault tolerance but can be costly and complex to implement.

To deploy a specific network topology, network administrators can use CLI commands to configure the

network devices accordingly. For example, to configure a star topology using Cisco switches, administrators can use the following commands:
csharpCopy code

enable configure terminal interface <interface> switchport mode access switchport access vlan <vlan ID>

In this command sequence, "interface <interface>" specifies the switch port to be configured, "switchport mode access" sets the port to be an access port, and "switchport access vlan <vlan ID>" assigns the port to the specified VLAN. By repeating these commands for each switch port, administrators can create a star topology where all devices are connected to a central switch.

Another important consideration in LAN design is network segmentation, which involves dividing the LAN into smaller, more manageable segments called subnets or VLANs. Network segmentation helps improve performance, security, and manageability by isolating traffic and controlling access between different parts of the network. VLANs, in particular, are commonly used for network segmentation in LANs. VLANs enable network administrators to logically group devices based on criteria such as department, function, or security requirements, regardless of their physical location.

To configure VLANs for network segmentation, administrators can use CLI commands to create VLANs and assign switch ports to VLANs as described earlier. Additionally, inter-VLAN routing may be required to enable communication between VLANs. This can be achieved by configuring a router or Layer 3 switch to route traffic between VLANs using subinterfaces or virtual routing and forwarding (VRF) instances.

Addressing schemes are another important aspect of LAN design. IP addressing is used to uniquely identify devices on the network and facilitate communication between them. When designing LANs, administrators must carefully plan IP addressing schemes to ensure efficient allocation of IP addresses and minimize conflicts. This may involve selecting appropriate IP address ranges, subnetting, and implementing dynamic IP address assignment mechanisms such as DHCP (Dynamic Host Configuration Protocol).

To configure IP addressing on LAN devices, administrators can use CLI commands to assign IP addresses and subnet masks to interfaces. For example, on a Cisco router, the following commands can be used to configure IP addressing on an interface:

csharpCopy code

```
enable configure terminal interface <interface> ip
address <ip address> <subnet mask> no shutdown
```

In this command sequence, "interface <interface>" specifies the router interface to be configured, "ip address <ip address> <subnet mask>" assigns an IP address and subnet mask to the interface, and "no shutdown" enables the interface. By repeating these commands for each router interface, administrators can configure IP addressing for LAN devices.

Cabling infrastructure is another critical consideration in LAN design. The physical cabling infrastructure forms the backbone of the LAN, providing connectivity between network devices. When designing LANs, administrators must select appropriate cabling types, such as twisted pair copper cabling (e.g., Cat 5e, Cat 6) or fiber optic cabling, based on factors such as bandwidth requirements, distance limitations, and environmental conditions. Additionally, proper cable management practices should be followed to ensure neat and organized cabling installations that facilitate maintenance and troubleshooting.

Finally, network equipment selection plays a vital role in LAN design. The selection of network devices such as switches, routers, access points, and firewalls depends on factors such as performance requirements, scalability, feature set, and budget constraints. For example, in a high-performance LAN environment, administrators may choose enterprise-grade switches with advanced features such as Layer 3 routing, Quality of Service (QoS), and Power over Ethernet (PoE) support. Similarly, in a wireless LAN (WLAN) deployment, administrators may select access points that support the latest Wi-Fi standards and offer features such as centralized management and rogue AP detection.

By carefully considering these LAN design considerations and deploying appropriate configurations using CLI commands or graphical user interfaces (GUIs), network administrators can design LANs that meet the performance, reliability, and security requirements of their organizations. A well-designed LAN provides a solid foundation for supporting critical business applications, enabling efficient communication and collaboration among users and ensuring seamless access to network resources.

LAN setup involves a series of steps to establish a local area network (LAN) infrastructure that facilitates communication and resource sharing among devices within a confined geographical area. These steps encompass various tasks, including network planning, physical setup, configuration of network devices, and testing to ensure proper functionality.

The first step in LAN setup is planning, which involves defining the scope and requirements of the network. Network planners must assess the number of users and devices expected to connect to the LAN, determine the types of applications and services that will be used, and identify any special considerations such as security or scalability requirements. Additionally, planners must decide on the network topology, addressing scheme, and cabling infrastructure to be used.

Once the planning phase is complete, the next step is to physically set up the LAN infrastructure. This involves installing network devices such as switches, routers, access points, and cabling infrastructure. Network devices should be strategically placed to ensure optimal coverage and connectivity throughout the LAN. Cable runs should be neatly organized and labeled to facilitate maintenance and troubleshooting in the future.

To configure network devices such as switches and routers, network administrators can use CLI commands or graphical user interfaces (GUIs) provided by the device manufacturer. For example, to configure basic settings on a Cisco switch, administrators can use the following CLI commands:

```csharp
csharpCopy code
enable configure terminal hostname <hostname>
interface <interface> switchport mode access
switchport access vlan <vlan ID> no shutdown
```

In this command sequence, "enable" enters privileged EXEC mode, "configure terminal" enters global configuration mode, "hostname <hostname>" sets the hostname of the switch, "interface <interface>" specifies the switch port to be configured, "switchport mode access" sets the port to be an access port, "switchport access vlan <vlan ID>" assigns the port to the specified VLAN, and "no shutdown" enables the interface. By repeating these commands for each switch port, administrators can configure basic settings for the LAN.

After configuring network devices, administrators must verify the connectivity and functionality of the LAN. This can be done by testing network connectivity between devices, verifying that devices can access network resources such as file shares and printers, and testing the performance of the network using tools such as ping, traceroute, and bandwidth testing utilities.

Security is another important consideration in LAN setup. Administrators must implement security measures to protect the LAN from unauthorized access, data breaches, and network attacks. This may involve configuring features such as port security, VLANs, access control lists (ACLs), and firewall rules to control access to network resources and mitigate potential threats.

To configure port security on a Cisco switch, administrators can use the following CLI command: csharpCopy code

```
interface <interface> switchport port-security
switchport port-security mac-address <mac
address>
```

In this command sequence, "interface <interface>" specifies the switch port to be configured for port security, "switchport port-security" enables port security on the interface, and "switchport port-security mac-address <mac address>" specifies the MAC address of the authorized device. Multiple MAC addresses can be configured for each switch port, allowing multiple devices to connect to the port.

Similarly, VLANs can be used to segment the LAN and control access between different parts of the network. Administrators can use the following CLI commands to create VLANs and assign switch ports to VLANs: phpCopy code

```
configure terminal vlan <vlan ID> name <vlan name>
exit interface <interface> switchport mode access
switchport access vlan <vlan ID> exit
```

In this command sequence, "configure terminal" enters global configuration mode, "vlan <vlan ID>" creates a new VLAN with the specified VLAN ID, "name <vlan name>" assigns a name to the VLAN for easier identification, "interface <interface>" specifies the switch port to be configured, "switchport mode access" sets the port to be an access port, and "switchport access vlan <vlan ID>" assigns the port to the specified VLAN. By repeating these commands for each switch port, administrators can configure VLANs for network segmentation.

Overall, LAN setup involves a series of steps to plan, deploy, configure, and secure a local area network. By following these steps and using CLI commands or GUIs provided by network devices, administrators can establish LAN infrastructure that provides reliable connectivity, efficient resource sharing, and robust security for users and applications.

Chapter 8: Exploring Wireless Networking Concepts

Wireless standards and technologies are foundational elements in modern networking, facilitating wireless communication and connectivity across a wide range of devices and applications. These standards and technologies define the specifications and protocols for wireless communication, enabling interoperability, performance, and security in wireless networks. From the early days of wireless communication to the latest advancements in wireless technologies, understanding these standards is essential for designing, deploying, and managing wireless networks effectively.

One of the earliest wireless standards is the IEEE 802.11 standard, which defines the specifications for wireless local area networks (WLANs). The 802.11 standard has evolved over the years to support higher data rates, increased range, and improved security. The original 802.11 standard, released in 1997, supported data rates of up to 2 Mbps in the 2.4 GHz frequency band. Subsequent revisions of the standard, such as 802.11b, 802.11g, and 802.11n, introduced improvements in data rates and compatibility with legacy devices. For example, the 802.11b standard, released in 1999, increased the maximum data rate to 11 Mbps, while the 802.11g standard, released in 2003, further increased the data rate to 54 Mbps.

To deploy a wireless network using the 802.11 standard, network administrators can use access points (APs) and wireless clients that support the standard. Configuration of wireless APs typically involves setting parameters such as the SSID (Service Set Identifier), security settings (e.g., WPA2-PSK), and radio channels. For example, to configure basic settings on a Cisco wireless AP, administrators can use the following CLI commands:

```csharp
enable configure terminal interface dot11radio 0 ssid <ssid> encryption mode <encryption mode> encryption key <key> channel <channel> exit
```

In this command sequence, "enable" enters privileged EXEC mode, "configure terminal" enters global configuration mode, "interface dot11radio 0" specifies the wireless radio interface to be configured, "ssid <ssid>" sets the SSID of the wireless network, "encryption mode <encryption mode>" specifies the encryption mode (e.g., WPA2), "encryption key <key>" sets the encryption key, and "channel <channel>" sets the radio channel.

As wireless technology continued to evolve, newer standards such as 802.11ac and 802.11ax were introduced to meet the growing demand for higher data rates, increased capacity, and improved performance. The 802.11ac standard, also known as Wi-Fi 5, was released in 2013 and introduced features such as multi-user MIMO (Multiple Input Multiple Output), wider channels (up to 160 MHz), and higher-order modulation (up to 256-QAM), enabling data rates of up to several gigabits per second. The 802.11ax standard, also known as Wi-Fi 6, builds upon the capabilities of 802.11ac and introduces additional features such as OFDMA

(Orthogonal Frequency Division Multiple Access), MU-MIMO with uplink support, and improved efficiency in dense deployment scenarios.

To deploy a wireless network using the 802.11ac or 802.11ax standard, network administrators can use access points and wireless clients that support these standards. Configuration of wireless APs for these standards may involve setting additional parameters such as channel width, transmit power, and beamforming. For example, to configure basic settings on a Cisco wireless AP for 802.11ac or 802.11ax, administrators can use similar CLI commands as described earlier, with additional options for configuring advanced features.

In addition to the IEEE 802.11 standards, other wireless technologies and standards have emerged to address specific use cases and requirements. For example, Bluetooth is a wireless technology standard for short-range communication between devices, commonly used for connecting peripherals such as keyboards, mice, and headphones to computers and mobile devices. Zigbee is another wireless technology standard for low-power, low-data-rate communication in applications such as home automation, industrial control, and wireless sensor networks.

To deploy Bluetooth or Zigbee networks, network administrators can use devices that support these standards and configure them according to the specific requirements of the application. For example, configuring Bluetooth devices may involve pairing devices, setting device visibility, and configuring security settings such as passkeys. For Zigbee devices, administrators may need to configure network parameters such as PAN ID (Personal Area Network Identifier) and channel selection.

Overall, wireless standards and technologies play a critical role in enabling wireless communication and connectivity in modern networks. By understanding these standards and technologies and deploying them effectively using appropriate configurations and techniques, network administrators can build robust and high-performance wireless networks that meet the needs of their organizations and users.

Wireless security measures are essential components of modern network infrastructure, ensuring the confidentiality, integrity, and availability of wireless communication and data transmission. As wireless networks continue to proliferate and become integral to business operations and personal connectivity, implementing robust security measures is paramount to mitigate the risks of unauthorized access, data breaches, and network attacks. Wireless security encompasses various techniques, protocols, and best practices to protect wireless networks from potential threats and vulnerabilities, safeguarding sensitive information and preserving the trust and integrity of the network environment.

One of the fundamental aspects of wireless security is encryption, which scrambles data transmitted over the wireless network to prevent unauthorized interception and eavesdropping. The most widely used encryption protocols for wireless networks are WEP (Wired Equivalent Privacy), WPA (Wi-Fi Protected Access), and WPA2. WEP, although widely deployed in the past, is now considered insecure due to vulnerabilities that can be exploited to decrypt data. WPA and WPA2 provide stronger security by using more robust encryption algorithms and implementing additional security features such as TKIP (Temporal Key Integrity Protocol) and AES (Advanced Encryption Standard).

To configure WPA or WPA2 encryption on a wireless network, network administrators can use CLI commands or graphical user interfaces (GUIs) provided by wireless access points (APs) or wireless routers. For example, to configure WPA2 encryption on a Cisco wireless AP, administrators can use the following CLI commands:

vbnetCopy code

```
enable configure terminal interface dot11radio 0
encryption mode ciphers aes-ccm ssid <ssid> wpa-psk
ascii <pre-shared-key> exit
```

In this command sequence, "enable" enters privileged EXEC mode, "configure terminal" enters global configuration mode, "interface dot11radio 0" specifies the wireless radio interface to be configured, "encryption mode ciphers aes-ccm" selects the AES encryption algorithm, "ssid <ssid>" sets the SSID of the wireless network, and "wpa-psk ascii <pre-shared-key>" specifies the pre-shared key for WPA2 encryption.

Another important wireless security measure is authentication, which verifies the identity of users and devices before granting access to the wireless network. Authentication can be implemented using various methods, including pre-shared keys (PSKs), 802.1X/EAP (Extensible Authentication Protocol), and MAC address filtering. Pre-shared keys are commonly used in small-scale deployments and home networks, where a single passphrase is shared among all users to authenticate to the network.

To configure MAC address filtering on a wireless network, administrators can use CLI commands or GUIs provided by wireless APs or routers. For example, to configure MAC address filtering on a Cisco wireless AP, administrators can use the following CLI commands:

vbnetCopy code

```
enable configure terminal interface dot11radio 0 mac-address-table static <mac-address> <interface> exit
```

In this command sequence, "enable" enters privileged EXEC mode, "configure terminal" enters global configuration mode, "interface dot11radio 0" specifies the wireless radio interface to be configured, "mac-address-table static <mac-address> <interface>" adds a static entry to the MAC address table, specifying the MAC address of the authorized device and the interface to which it is connected.

Additionally, network administrators can enhance wireless security by implementing intrusion detection and prevention systems (IDS/IPS), which monitor wireless traffic for suspicious activity and automatically take action to block or mitigate potential threats. IDS/IPS systems can detect common wireless attacks such as rogue APs, deauthentication attacks, and man-in-the-middle attacks, helping to maintain the security and integrity of the wireless network.

To deploy an IDS/IPS system for wireless security, administrators can use dedicated hardware appliances or software-based solutions that integrate with existing network infrastructure. These systems typically require configuration of detection policies, alert thresholds, and response actions to effectively monitor and protect the wireless network from potential threats.

In summary, wireless security measures are critical for protecting wireless networks from potential threats and vulnerabilities. By implementing robust encryption, authentication, access control, and intrusion detection/prevention mechanisms, network administrators can ensure the confidentiality, integrity, and availability of wireless communication and data transmission. By using CLI commands or GUIs provided by network devices and security appliances, administrators can configure and deploy these security measures effectively to safeguard wireless networks against evolving security threats and attacks.

Chapter 9: Network Security Fundamentals

Common network security threats pose significant risks to the confidentiality, integrity, and availability of data and resources within network environments. Understanding these threats is essential for network administrators and security professionals to implement effective countermeasures and protect against potential breaches and attacks. From malicious software and unauthorized access attempts to social engineering tactics and insider threats, a wide range of threats can compromise the security of networks and undermine the trust and reliability of network infrastructure.

One of the most prevalent network security threats is malware, malicious software designed to disrupt, damage, or gain unauthorized access to computer systems and networks. Malware includes various types such as viruses, worms, Trojans, ransomware, and spyware, each with distinct characteristics and attack vectors. Viruses are programs that replicate themselves and spread to other computers through infected files or email attachments, while worms are self-replicating programs that spread across networks without requiring user intervention. Trojans, on the other hand, masquerade as legitimate software to deceive users into executing them, allowing attackers to gain unauthorized access or steal sensitive information.

To protect against malware threats, network administrators can deploy antivirus software and intrusion prevention systems (IPS) that monitor network traffic for malicious activity and block or quarantine suspicious files and connections. Additionally, regular software updates and patches should be applied to systems and devices to address known vulnerabilities and reduce the risk of exploitation by malware.

Another common network security threat is unauthorized access, which occurs when individuals or entities gain unauthorized access to network resources or sensitive information. Unauthorized access can result from weak or default passwords, misconfigured access controls, or exploitation of software vulnerabilities. Attackers may use various techniques such as brute-force attacks, password guessing, or exploiting weak authentication mechanisms to gain unauthorized access to network devices, servers, or databases.

To mitigate the risk of unauthorized access, network administrators can implement strong authentication mechanisms such as multi-factor authentication (MFA) and enforce strict access control policies. This may involve configuring user accounts with complex passwords, regularly reviewing and updating access permissions, and implementing role-based access control (RBAC) to limit privileges based on user roles and responsibilities. Additionally, network devices such as routers, switches, and firewalls should be configured to log and monitor access attempts, allowing administrators to identify and respond to unauthorized access events promptly.

Social engineering is another significant network security threat that exploits human psychology to manipulate individuals into divulging confidential information or performing actions that compromise security. Social engineering techniques include phishing, pretexting, baiting, and tailgating, among others, which rely on deception, manipulation, and persuasion to trick users into revealing sensitive information or granting access to network resources.

To combat social engineering attacks, organizations should invest in employee education and awareness training to recognize and resist social engineering tactics. Employees should be trained to verify the identity of individuals requesting access to sensitive information or restricted areas, scrutinize email messages and attachments for signs of phishing or malware, and report suspicious activities or requests to the appropriate authorities. Additionally, organizations can implement email filtering and content scanning solutions to detect and block phishing emails and other malicious content before reaching end users.

Insider threats pose a significant risk to network security, as malicious insiders or negligent employees may intentionally or unintentionally compromise the confidentiality, integrity, or availability of data and resources. Insider threats can take various forms, including data theft, sabotage, fraud, and compliance violations, and may result from disgruntled employees, careless actions, or insufficient training and oversight.

To address insider threats, organizations should implement security controls and monitoring mechanisms to detect and prevent unauthorized activities by insiders. This may involve implementing data loss prevention (DLP) solutions to monitor and control the flow of sensitive data, implementing access controls and segregation of duties to limit privileges and reduce the risk of abuse, and conducting regular security awareness training and employee monitoring to detect and deter malicious insider behavior.

In summary, common network security threats pose significant risks to organizations and individuals, threatening the confidentiality, integrity, and availability of data and resources within network environments. By understanding these threats and implementing appropriate security measures and countermeasures, network administrators and security professionals can effectively mitigate the risk of breaches and attacks, safeguarding the integrity and reliability of network infrastructure and protecting sensitive information from unauthorized access or disclosure.

Basic security measures and best practices are essential elements in safeguarding computer systems, networks, and data against various threats and vulnerabilities. These measures encompass a wide range of techniques, policies, and procedures aimed at reducing risk, improving resilience, and enhancing the overall security posture of organizations and individuals. From implementing strong passwords and access controls to regularly updating software and conducting security awareness training, adhering to basic security practices is critical for mitigating common security risks and protecting against potential breaches and attacks.

One of the fundamental security measures is the implementation of strong passwords, which serve as the first line of defense against unauthorized access to computer systems and accounts. Strong passwords should be complex, unique, and difficult to guess, typically comprising a combination of uppercase and lowercase letters, numbers, and special characters. Additionally, passwords should be regularly updated and not reused across multiple accounts to minimize the risk of compromise in the event of a data breach.

To enforce strong password policies, organizations can use group policy settings in Windows environments or configuration commands in Linux environments to set password complexity requirements, enforce password expiration, and enforce account lockout thresholds. For example, in a Windows Active Directory environment, administrators can use the following command to configure password complexity requirements:

bashCopy code

```
net accounts /minpwlen:8 /minpwage:1 /maxpwage:90 /minpwage:7 /uniquepw:10
```

In this command, "/minpwlen:8" specifies a minimum password length of 8 characters, "/minpwage:1" and "/maxpwage:90" specify minimum and maximum password ages of 1 and 90 days, respectively, and "/uniquepw:10" specifies that new passwords must differ from the previous 10 passwords.

Another critical security measure is access control, which involves managing and restricting access to sensitive resources and information based on user roles, permissions, and privileges. Access control mechanisms such as role-based access control (RBAC) and access control lists (ACLs) allow organizations to define and enforce granular access policies that limit access to authorized users and entities while preventing unauthorized access and data exposure.

To configure access control settings, administrators can use security group memberships in Windows environments or ACLs in Linux environments to define access permissions for files, folders, and network resources. For example, in a Linux environment, administrators can use the following command to set file permissions:

phpCopy code

```
chmod <permissions> <filename>
```

In this command, "<permissions>" specifies the desired access permissions (e.g., read, write, execute) in numeric or symbolic notation, and "<filename>" specifies the file or directory to which the permissions apply.

Regular software updates and patch management are also essential security measures to protect against known vulnerabilities and exploits. Software vendors release updates and patches to address security vulnerabilities, bugs, and performance issues discovered in their products. By regularly applying updates and patches to operating systems, applications, and firmware, organizations can minimize the risk of exploitation by malware, hackers, and other attackers seeking to exploit known vulnerabilities.

To manage software updates and patches, organizations can use automated patch management tools or configuration management systems to deploy updates and patches across multiple systems efficiently. For example, in a Windows environment, administrators can use Windows Server Update Services (WSUS) or Group Policy to centrally manage and deploy updates to Windows clients and servers. In a Linux environment, administrators can use package management tools such as apt, yum, or zypper to install updates and patches for Linux distributions.

Security awareness training is another critical component of basic security measures, as human error and negligence are significant contributors to security breaches and incidents. Educating employees and end users about security best practices, phishing awareness, social engineering tactics, and incident reporting procedures can help raise awareness and foster a culture of security within organizations. Training programs should be tailored to the specific needs and risks of the organization, covering topics such as password security, data protection, safe browsing habits, and response to security incidents.

To conduct security awareness training, organizations can use a combination of online training modules, instructor-led sessions, simulated phishing exercises, and periodic security reminders to reinforce key concepts and promote a security-conscious mindset among employees. Training programs should be regularly updated to address emerging threats and trends in cybersecurity and should be mandatory for all employees, contractors, and third-party vendors with access to sensitive information and systems.

In summary, basic security measures and best practices are essential for protecting computer systems, networks, and data against a wide range of threats and vulnerabilities. By implementing strong passwords, access controls, software updates, and security awareness training, organizations can strengthen their security posture and reduce the risk of security breaches and incidents. Additionally, regular security assessments and audits can help identify weaknesses and gaps in security controls, allowing organizations to take proactive steps to address vulnerabilities and improve overall security readiness.

Chapter 10: Troubleshooting Common Network Issues

Network troubleshooting methodologies are systematic approaches used to identify, diagnose, and resolve issues affecting the performance, connectivity, and reliability of computer networks. These methodologies encompass a series of steps and techniques designed to isolate problems, analyze root causes, and implement corrective actions to restore normal network operation. From gathering information and identifying symptoms to testing hypotheses and implementing solutions, effective network troubleshooting requires a combination of technical expertise, critical thinking, and problem-solving skills.

The first step in network troubleshooting is gathering information and identifying symptoms, which involves gathering relevant data about the network environment, symptoms reported by users, and any recent changes or events that may have preceded the issue. Network administrators can use various tools and techniques to collect information, including network monitoring tools, syslog messages, and user reports. By analyzing network traffic, performance metrics, and error logs, administrators can identify patterns and anomalies that may indicate the presence of a problem.

Once symptoms are identified, the next step is to define the problem and establish a hypothesis based on the available information. This involves formulating a hypothesis or educated guess about the possible cause of the issue, taking into account factors such as network topology, configuration settings, and hardware/software components. For example, if users are reporting slow network performance, the hypothesis may be that there is congestion on the network or a problem with a specific device or interface.

To validate the hypothesis and narrow down the scope of the problem, network administrators can use diagnostic tools and techniques to gather additional data and perform targeted tests. This may involve using ping and traceroute commands to test connectivity and measure latency, performing packet captures to analyze network traffic, and checking device configurations for errors or misconfigurations. By systematically testing different components of the network, administrators can gather evidence to support or refute the initial hypothesis and identify the root cause of the problem.

For example, to perform a traceroute test to diagnose network connectivity issues, administrators can use the following command:

phpCopy code

```
traceroute <destination>
```

In this command, "<destination>" specifies the IP address or hostname of the target device or destination. Once the root cause of the problem is identified, the next step is to develop and implement a solution to resolve the issue. This may involve reconfiguring network devices, updating firmware or software, replacing faulty hardware components, or implementing workaround solutions to mitigate the impact of the problem. Network administrators should carefully assess the potential impact of proposed solutions and consider factors such as cost, feasibility, and potential risks before implementing changes to the network infrastructure.

After implementing the solution, administrators should verify and test the changes to ensure that the problem has been resolved and that normal network operation has been restored. This may involve conducting additional tests and monitoring network performance to confirm that symptoms have been alleviated and that the network is functioning as expected. In some cases, it may be necessary to communicate with users or stakeholders to inform them of the resolution and any necessary follow-up actions.

Throughout the troubleshooting process, documentation is essential to keep track of the steps taken, observations made, and solutions implemented. Network administrators should maintain detailed records of troubleshooting activities, including timestamps, commands executed, and outcomes of tests and changes. This documentation not only helps in tracking the progress of troubleshooting efforts but also serves as a valuable resource for future reference and knowledge sharing.

In addition to reactive troubleshooting, proactive measures such as preventive maintenance and performance monitoring can help identify and address potential issues before they impact network operations. Regular audits, security assessments, and vulnerability scans can help identify weaknesses and vulnerabilities in the network infrastructure, allowing administrators to take proactive steps to mitigate risks and strengthen security.

In summary, network troubleshooting methodologies are systematic approaches used to diagnose and resolve issues affecting the performance, connectivity, and reliability of computer networks. By following a structured process of gathering information, defining problems, testing hypotheses, and implementing solutions, network administrators can effectively identify and resolve network issues, minimize downtime, and ensure the smooth operation of network infrastructure. Through proactive measures and continuous improvement, organizations can enhance the resilience and reliability of their networks and minimize the impact of potential disruptions on business operations.

Common network issue resolution techniques are essential skills for network administrators and IT professionals tasked with maintaining the performance, reliability, and security of computer networks. These techniques encompass a variety of troubleshooting strategies, diagnostic tools, and problem-solving methodologies used to identify, diagnose, and resolve issues affecting network connectivity, performance, and functionality. From basic connectivity problems and configuration errors to more complex issues such as network congestion and security breaches, network administrators must be proficient in applying a range of techniques to effectively address common network issues and ensure the smooth operation of network infrastructure.

One of the most fundamental network issue resolution techniques is verifying network connectivity, which involves confirming that devices can communicate with each other and access network resources. Administrators can use the ping command to test connectivity to a specific device or IP address, sending ICMP (Internet Control Message Protocol) echo requests and waiting for ICMP echo replies to confirm that packets are being successfully transmitted and received. For example, to ping a device with IP address 192.168.1.1, administrators can use the following command:

Copy code

ping 192.168.1.1

In addition to ping, administrators can use traceroute to identify the path that packets take to reach a destination device, helping to pinpoint potential connectivity issues such as network congestion or routing problems. By analyzing the output of traceroute, administrators can identify hops or routers along the path where packet loss or delays occur, allowing them to take corrective action to resolve connectivity issues.

Another common network issue resolution technique is checking network configuration settings, which involves reviewing the configuration of network devices such as routers, switches, and firewalls to identify errors or misconfigurations that may be causing issues. Administrators can use CLI commands or management interfaces to access device configurations and verify settings such as IP addresses, subnet masks, gateway addresses, VLAN configurations, and access control lists (ACLs). For example, to view the configuration of a Cisco router, administrators can use the following command: arduinoCopy code

show running-config

By reviewing the configuration settings of network devices, administrators can identify discrepancies between the intended configuration and the actual configuration, allowing them to correct errors and ensure that devices are properly configured for optimal network performance and security.

Performance monitoring is another important network issue resolution technique, which involves continuously monitoring network traffic, resource utilization, and performance metrics to identify potential issues and bottlenecks before they impact network performance. Administrators can use network monitoring tools such as SNMP (Simple Network Management Protocol) monitoring software, packet analyzers, and bandwidth monitoring tools to collect and analyze data on network traffic, device status, and performance indicators such as latency, throughput, and packet loss.

By monitoring performance metrics over time, administrators can detect trends and anomalies that may indicate performance degradation or impending issues, allowing them to take proactive measures to address issues before they escalate. For example, administrators may notice a sudden increase in network traffic or packet loss during peak usage hours, indicating network congestion or bandwidth limitations. By identifying the cause of the performance degradation, administrators can implement solutions such as optimizing network configurations, upgrading hardware, or implementing quality of service (QoS) policies to prioritize critical traffic and ensure optimal network performance.

Security auditing and vulnerability scanning are essential network issue resolution techniques used to identify and address security vulnerabilities, weaknesses, and compliance issues within network infrastructure. Administrators can use vulnerability scanning tools and security assessment frameworks to scan network devices, servers, and applications for known vulnerabilities, misconfigurations, and security weaknesses that could be exploited by attackers. By identifying and addressing vulnerabilities proactively, administrators can reduce the risk of security breaches, data leaks, and other security incidents that could compromise the integrity and confidentiality of network resources.

For example, administrators can use vulnerability scanning tools such as Nessus, OpenVAS, or Qualys to scan network devices and servers for known vulnerabilities and security weaknesses. These tools generate reports highlighting vulnerabilities, severity levels, and recommended remediation steps, allowing administrators to prioritize and address issues based on their risk levels and potential impact on network security.

In summary, common network issue resolution techniques are essential skills for network administrators and IT professionals responsible for maintaining the performance, reliability, and security of computer networks. By leveraging techniques such as verifying network connectivity, checking configuration settings, monitoring performance metrics, and conducting security audits, administrators can effectively identify, diagnose, and resolve common network issues, ensuring the smooth operation of network infrastructure and minimizing the impact of potential disruptions on business operations. Through proactive monitoring, continuous improvement, and adherence to best practices, organizations can enhance the resilience and reliability of their networks and mitigate the risk of network-related issues and security incidents.

BOOK 2
SWITCHING STRATEGIES
INTERMEDIATE TECHNIQUES FOR NETWORK OPTIMIZATION

ROB BOTWRIGHT

Chapter 1: Understanding VLANs (Virtual Local Area Networks)

VLAN (Virtual Local Area Network) concepts and benefits are fundamental to modern network design and management, offering numerous advantages in terms of scalability, security, and network segmentation. VLANs are virtual networks created within a physical network infrastructure, allowing administrators to logically segment network traffic and isolate devices into separate broadcast domains, regardless of their physical location or connectivity. By implementing VLANs, organizations can improve network performance, enhance security, and simplify network management, resulting in a more efficient and flexible network infrastructure.

The VLAN concept revolves around the idea of logically dividing a single physical network into multiple virtual networks, each with its own broadcast domain. This segmentation is achieved by assigning VLAN tags to network traffic, indicating which VLAN a particular packet belongs to. VLAN tags are inserted into the Ethernet frame header, allowing switches to identify and forward traffic to the appropriate VLAN based on the VLAN ID. This enables administrators to create distinct broadcast domains within a single physical network infrastructure, reducing network congestion, improving bandwidth utilization, and enhancing overall network performance.

One of the key benefits of VLANs is network segmentation, which allows administrators to partition the network into smaller, more manageable segments based on factors such as department, function, or security requirements. By segregating network traffic into separate VLANs, organizations can isolate sensitive or critical resources from non-essential traffic, reducing the risk of unauthorized access, data breaches, and network attacks. For example, organizations can create separate VLANs for finance, HR, and engineering departments, ensuring that each department's traffic remains isolated and secure from other parts of the network.

To deploy VLANs, administrators must configure VLAN settings on network switches using CLI commands or graphical management interfaces. The first step is to define VLANs and assign VLAN IDs, which are numerical identifiers used to differentiate between different VLANs. For example, to create a VLAN with ID 100 on a Cisco Catalyst switch, administrators can use the following command:

arduinoCopy code

```
switch(config)# vlan 100
```

Once VLANs are created, administrators must assign switch ports to the appropriate VLANs using port-based VLAN assignments. This involves configuring switch ports to be members of specific VLANs, allowing devices connected to those ports to communicate within the assigned VLAN. For example, to assign a switch port to VLAN 100, administrators can use the following command:

```
arduinoCopy code
switch (config)#        interface        GigabitEthernet0/1
switch (config- if )#      switchport      mode      access
switch (config- if )# switchport access vlan 100
```

By configuring VLAN memberships on switch ports, administrators can control which devices belong to which VLANs, ensuring that network traffic remains segregated and secure according to organizational requirements.

In addition to network segmentation, VLANs offer benefits in terms of scalability and flexibility, allowing organizations to adapt and expand their network infrastructure to meet changing business needs. VLANs provide a scalable solution for adding new devices, departments, or locations to the network without the need for physical rewiring or reconfiguration. Administrators can simply create new VLANs and assign switch ports accordingly, enabling seamless integration of new devices or users into the existing network infrastructure.

Furthermore, VLANs facilitate network optimization and resource allocation by enabling administrators to prioritize traffic and implement quality of service (QoS) policies based on VLAN memberships. By assigning different traffic types to separate VLANs and applying QoS policies, organizations can ensure that critical applications receive priority access to network resources, while non-essential traffic is appropriately throttled or restricted. This helps improve overall network performance and user experience, particularly in environments with high network traffic or bandwidth-intensive applications.

Another benefit of VLANs is simplified network management, as administrators can configure and manage VLANs centrally from network switches or management platforms. VLAN configurations can be stored and managed centrally on network switches or in network management software, allowing administrators to easily modify VLAN settings, add or remove VLANs, and troubleshoot VLAN-related issues from a single interface. This centralized management approach streamlines network administration tasks, reduces the risk of configuration errors, and improves overall network efficiency and reliability.

In summary, VLAN concepts and benefits play a critical role in modern network design and management, offering advantages in terms of network segmentation, scalability, security, and simplified management. By implementing VLANs, organizations can create logical network segments to isolate traffic, improve performance, enhance security, and streamline network management. Through careful planning, configuration, and monitoring, administrators can leverage VLANs to build flexible, resilient, and efficient network infrastructures that meet the evolving needs of modern businesses.

VLAN configuration best practices are essential guidelines for network administrators and IT professionals tasked with designing, implementing, and managing VLANs in enterprise network environments.

These best practices encompass a range of recommendations and principles aimed at ensuring the effective deployment, security, and optimization of VLANs to support organizational requirements and objectives. By following VLAN configuration best practices, organizations can minimize security risks, optimize network performance, and simplify network management, resulting in a more robust and efficient network infrastructure.

One of the fundamental best practices in VLAN configuration is proper planning and design, which involves carefully defining VLANs based on organizational requirements, network topology, and security policies. Administrators should conduct a thorough assessment of the network environment to identify logical segmentation requirements, such as departmental boundaries, application requirements, and security zones. By defining VLANs based on these criteria, organizations can create a logical network structure that aligns with business needs and facilitates efficient traffic management and isolation.

Once VLANs are defined, administrators should establish clear naming conventions and numbering schemes to ensure consistency and clarity in VLAN identification and management. VLAN names should reflect their purpose or function, making it easier for administrators to understand their role within the network. Additionally, VLAN IDs should be carefully assigned to avoid conflicts and overlaps, with reserved ranges allocated for specific purposes such as management VLANs or native VLANs.

To configure VLANs on network switches, administrators can use CLI commands or graphical management interfaces provided by the switch vendor. The first step is to create VLANs and assign VLAN IDs, using commands such as "vlan" in Cisco IOS or "vlan database" in older Cisco switches. For example, to create a VLAN with ID 10 named "Finance," administrators can use the following command:

arduinoCopy code

```
switch(config)# vlan 10 switch(config-vlan)# name Finance
```

After creating VLANs, administrators should assign switch ports to the appropriate VLANs using port-based VLAN assignments. This involves configuring switch ports to be members of specific VLANs, allowing devices connected to those ports to communicate within the assigned VLAN. For example, to assign a switch port to VLAN 10, administrators can use the following command:

arduinoCopy code

```
switch(config)# interface GigabitEthernet0/1
switch(config-if)# switchport mode access
switch(config-if)# switchport access vlan 10
```

By configuring VLAN memberships on switch ports, administrators can control which devices belong to which VLANs, ensuring proper segmentation and traffic isolation.

Another important best practice in VLAN configuration is VLAN pruning, which involves restricting VLAN traffic to only those switches and ports where it is necessary.

VLAN pruning helps optimize network bandwidth and reduce unnecessary traffic by preventing VLAN traffic from traversing switches and ports where it is not required. Administrators can enable VLAN pruning on trunk links using commands such as "switchport trunk pruning vlan" in Cisco IOS. For example, to enable VLAN pruning on a trunk link, administrators can use the following command:

arduinoCopy code

```
switch(config-if)# switchport trunk pruning vlan remove <VLAN>
```

In this command, "<VLAN>" specifies the VLAN ID to be pruned from the trunk link.

Security is another critical aspect of VLAN configuration, and administrators should implement security measures to protect against unauthorized access and VLAN hopping attacks. One best practice is to enable port security features such as MAC address filtering and port security on switch ports to restrict access to authorized devices only. Administrators can use commands such as "switchport port-security" in Cisco IOS to configure port security settings. For example, to enable port security and restrict the maximum number of MAC addresses allowed on a switch port to 2, administrators can use the following command:

arduinoCopy code

```
switch(config-if)# switchport port-security
switch(config-if)# switchport port-security maximum 2
```

Additionally, administrators should implement VLAN access control lists (VACLs) or VLAN-based firewall rules to control traffic between VLANs and enforce security policies. VACLs allow administrators to filter traffic based on VLAN memberships, source/destination IP addresses, or other criteria, providing granular control over traffic flow between VLANs.

Documentation and documentation are key best practices in VLAN configuration, ensuring that configurations are well-documented and easily accessible to network administrators and support personnel. Administrators should maintain detailed records of VLAN configurations, including VLAN names, VLAN IDs, assigned switch ports, and security settings. Additionally, administrators should document VLAN design considerations, such as VLAN segmentation criteria and naming conventions, to provide context and guidance for future network changes and expansions.

Regular monitoring and auditing of VLAN configurations are also important best practices to ensure that VLAN configurations remain accurate, compliant, and optimized over time. Administrators should regularly review VLAN configurations, audit VLAN memberships and access controls, and identify any discrepancies or security vulnerabilities that may require remediation. By proactively monitoring VLAN configurations, organizations can identify and address issues before they impact network performance or security.

In summary, VLAN configuration best practices are essential guidelines for designing, implementing, and managing VLANs in enterprise network environments. By following best practices such as proper planning and design, clear naming conventions, VLAN pruning, security implementation, documentation, and monitoring, organizations can optimize VLAN configurations for performance, security, and manageability. Through careful adherence to best practices, administrators can ensure the effectiveness and reliability of VLANs in supporting organizational goals and objectives.

Chapter 2: Implementing Spanning Tree Protocol (STP)

STP (Spanning Tree Protocol) fundamentals and operation are essential components of network design and management, providing a mechanism for loop prevention and redundancy management in Ethernet networks. STP is a Layer 2 protocol standardized by the IEEE 802.1D specification, designed to prevent the formation of loops in Ethernet networks by dynamically blocking redundant links and establishing a loop-free topology. Understanding STP fundamentals and its operation is crucial for network administrators and engineers to ensure the stability, resilience, and optimal performance of Ethernet networks.

STP operates by electing a root bridge and calculating the shortest path to the root bridge from each network switch, thereby determining the topology of the network and identifying redundant links that should be blocked to prevent loops. The root bridge is the central switch in the network topology, acting as the reference point for calculating the shortest path to all other switches. Each switch in the network participates in the STP election process, exchanging Bridge Protocol Data Units (BPDUs) with neighboring switches to determine the root bridge and establish the optimal path to reach it.

To deploy STP in a network, administrators must enable STP on network switches using CLI commands or graphical management interfaces provided by the switch vendor. The most commonly used version of STP is IEEE 802.1D STP, also known as Common Spanning Tree (CST). To enable STP on a Cisco Catalyst switch, administrators can use the following command:

arduinoCopy code

switch(config)# spanning-tree mode pvst

This command configures the switch to operate in Per-VLAN Spanning Tree (PVST) mode, which creates a separate instance of STP for each VLAN configured on the switch. PVST allows for finer granularity in loop prevention and redundancy management by treating each VLAN as a separate network segment.

Once STP is enabled, switches participate in the STP election process to determine the root bridge and calculate the shortest path to reach it. The root bridge election process is based on a combination of factors, including the bridge ID and the path cost to the root bridge. The bridge ID consists of a priority value and a MAC address, with the lowest bridge ID being elected as the root bridge. Administrators can manually configure the priority value to influence the root bridge election process, ensuring that a designated switch becomes the root bridge if desired.

After the root bridge is elected, each switch calculates the shortest path to reach the root bridge based on the path cost, which is determined by the speed of the links between switches. Lower-speed links have higher path costs, so switches prefer higher-speed links when calculating the shortest path to the root bridge. Once the shortest path is determined, switches identify and block redundant links that are not part of the shortest path, ensuring a loop-free topology and preventing broadcast storms and network congestion.

STP operates by exchanging BPDUs between switches to convey information about the network topology and synchronize the STP configuration. BPDUs contain information such as the bridge ID, root bridge ID, path cost, and port roles (e.g., root port, designated port, and blocked port). Switches use this information to make forwarding decisions and maintain a loop-free topology. If a switch detects a change in the network topology, such as the failure of a link or a switch, it propagates this information to other switches by sending BPDUs, allowing the network to dynamically adjust and maintain a stable topology.

In addition to IEEE 802.1D STP, there are several variations of STP that provide enhancements and optimizations for specific network environments. These include Rapid Spanning Tree Protocol (RSTP), which improves convergence time and provides faster link failover, and Multiple Spanning Tree Protocol (MSTP), which allows for the configuration of multiple spanning tree instances to support different VLANs or network segments. Administrators can choose the appropriate STP variant based on the specific requirements and characteristics of their network infrastructure.

In summary, STP fundamentals and operation are critical aspects of Ethernet network design and management, providing a mechanism for loop prevention and redundancy management. By understanding the principles of STP and deploying it effectively in network environments, administrators can ensure the stability, resilience, and optimal performance of Ethernet networks. Through proper configuration, monitoring, and maintenance of STP-enabled switches, organizations can build robust and reliable network infrastructures that meet the demands of modern business applications and services.

Configuring STP (Spanning Tree Protocol) for redundancy and loop prevention is a crucial aspect of network design and management, particularly in Ethernet networks where redundant links are commonly deployed to improve fault tolerance and network availability. STP is a Layer 2 protocol standardized by the IEEE 802.1D specification, designed to prevent the formation of loops in Ethernet networks by dynamically blocking redundant links and establishing a loop-free topology. By properly configuring STP, network administrators can ensure that redundant links are utilized efficiently while preventing loops and minimizing the risk of broadcast storms and network congestion.

The first step in configuring STP for redundancy and loop prevention is to enable STP on network switches using CLI commands or graphical management interfaces provided by the switch vendor. Most network switches support STP out of the box, but administrators may need to enable it manually and configure additional parameters to optimize its operation. To enable STP on a Cisco Catalyst switch, administrators can use the following command:

arduinoCopy code

switch(config)# spanning-tree mode pvst

This command configures the switch to operate in Per-VLAN Spanning Tree (PVST) mode, which creates a separate instance of STP for each VLAN configured on the switch. PVST allows for finer granularity in loop prevention and redundancy management by treating each VLAN as a separate network segment.

Once STP is enabled, switches participate in the STP election process to determine the root bridge and calculate the shortest path to reach it. The root bridge is the central switch in the network topology, acting as the reference point for calculating the shortest path to all other switches. The root bridge election process is based on a combination of factors, including the bridge ID and the path cost to the root bridge. The switch with the lowest bridge ID is elected as the root bridge.

Administrators can influence the root bridge election process by manually configuring the priority value of switches to ensure that a designated switch becomes the root bridge if desired. To configure the priority value of a switch, administrators can use the following command:

arduinoCopy code

```
switch(config)# spanning-tree vlan <VLAN> priority <priority-value>
```

In this command, "<VLAN>" specifies the VLAN for which the priority value is configured, and "<priority-value>" specifies the priority value assigned to the switch. Lower priority values indicate a higher priority for becoming the root bridge.

Once the root bridge is elected, each switch calculates the shortest path to reach the root bridge based on the path cost, which is determined by the speed of the links between switches. Lower-speed links have higher path costs, so switches prefer higher-speed links when calculating the shortest path to the root bridge. Once the shortest path is determined, switches identify and block redundant links that are not part of the shortest path, ensuring a loop-free topology and preventing broadcast storms and network congestion.

Another important aspect of configuring STP for redundancy and loop prevention is optimizing the STP configuration parameters to minimize convergence time and ensure rapid link failover in the event of a network change or failure. STP convergence time refers to the time it takes for the network to transition to a stable state after a topology change occurs, such as a link failure or switch reboot. By default, STP convergence time can be relatively slow, leading to network downtime and performance degradation during the convergence process.

To optimize STP convergence time, administrators can use enhancements such as Rapid Spanning Tree Protocol (RSTP) or Cisco's proprietary enhancements such as BackboneFast and UplinkFast. RSTP is an IEEE standard (802.1w) that provides faster convergence than traditional STP by reducing the number of states and timers used in the convergence process. To enable RSTP on a Cisco Catalyst switch, administrators can use the following command:

arduinoCopy code

```
switch(config)# spanning-tree mode rapid-pvst
```

This command configures the switch to operate in Rapid PVST+ mode, which enables RSTP for all VLANs configured on the switch. Rapid PVST+ provides faster convergence and improved link failover compared to traditional STP, helping to minimize network downtime and ensure rapid recovery from network failures.

Additionally, administrators can enable Cisco's proprietary enhancements such as BackboneFast and UplinkFast to further improve STP convergence time and link failover. BackboneFast allows non-root switches to quickly recompute the STP topology in response to a root bridge failure, while UplinkFast provides fast failover for blocked ports in the event of a link failure. To enable BackboneFast and UplinkFast on a Cisco Catalyst switch, administrators can use the following commands:

arduinoCopy code

```
switch(config)#        spanning-tree        backbonefast
switch(config)# spanning-tree uplinkfast
```

By configuring STP for redundancy and loop prevention and optimizing its configuration parameters, administrators can ensure the stability, resilience, and optimal performance of Ethernet networks. Through proper planning, deployment, and maintenance of STP-enabled switches, organizations can build robust and reliable network infrastructures that meet the demands of modern business applications and services.

Chapter 3: Inter-VLAN Routing Techniques

Router-on-a-Stick configuration is a technique used in computer networking to enable routing between multiple VLANs using a single physical router interface. This approach is particularly useful in environments where VLANs are deployed to segregate network traffic and provide logical segmentation, but a limited number of router interfaces are available for inter-VLAN routing. By leveraging Router-on-a-Stick configuration, network administrators can route traffic between VLANs efficiently and cost-effectively, without the need for dedicated router interfaces for each VLAN.

To deploy Router-on-a-Stick configuration, the first step is to configure the router interface connected to the switch as a trunk port, allowing it to carry traffic for multiple VLANs. Trunk ports support the transmission of traffic from multiple VLANs over a single physical link by encapsulating each frame with a VLAN tag that identifies its VLAN membership. This enables the router to differentiate between VLANs and route traffic accordingly.

On Cisco routers, the interface configuration command "interface <interface>" is used to access the interface configuration mode, where various parameters can be configured. To configure a router interface as a trunk port, administrators can use the following command: arduinoCopy code router(config)# interface <interface> router(config-if)# switchport mode trunk

This command sets the interface mode to trunk, allowing it to carry traffic for multiple VLANs.

Once the router interface is configured as a trunk port, the next step is to create and configure subinterfaces for each VLAN on the router. Subinterfaces are logical interfaces that are associated with a physical interface and are used to route traffic for specific VLANs. Each subinterface is configured with an IP address corresponding to the VLAN subnet and encapsulation settings that match the VLAN tagging used on the trunk link.

To create a subinterface on a Cisco router, administrators can use the following command:

arduinoCopy code

```
router(config)#      interface      <interface>.<vlan-id>
router(config-if)#   encapsulation  dot1q  <vlan-id>
router(config-if)#   ip address <ip-address> <subnet-mask>
```

In this command, "<interface>" specifies the physical interface name, "<vlan-id>" specifies the VLAN ID associated with the subinterface, "<ip-address>" specifies the IP address assigned to the subinterface, and "<subnet-mask>" specifies the subnet mask for the VLAN subnet.

For example, to create a subinterface for VLAN 10 with an IP address of 192.168.10.1/24 on interface GigabitEthernet0/0, administrators can use the following commands:

```
arduinoCopy code
router(config)#     interface     GigabitEthernet0/0.10
router(config-if)#    encapsulation     dot1q     10
router(config-if)#    ip     address     192.168.10.1
255.255.255.0
```
Once subinterfaces are configured for each VLAN, the router is able to route traffic between VLANs using the configured subinterfaces. Traffic arriving on the trunk link is tagged with VLAN IDs, allowing the router to route traffic to the appropriate subinterface based on the VLAN membership of each frame.

Router-on-a-Stick configuration offers several advantages, including efficient utilization of router interfaces, simplified network design, and flexibility in VLAN deployment. By using a single router interface to route traffic for multiple VLANs, organizations can reduce hardware costs and complexity associated with deploying dedicated router interfaces for each VLAN. Additionally, Router-on-a-Stick configuration simplifies network design by centralizing inter-VLAN routing on a single router, making it easier to manage and troubleshoot network connectivity.

Furthermore, Router-on-a-Stick configuration provides flexibility in VLAN deployment, allowing administrators to easily add or remove VLANs and adjust routing configurations as network requirements change. This flexibility enables organizations to adapt their network infrastructure to evolving business needs and scale network resources efficiently.

However, it's important to consider potential limitations and scalability issues when deploying Router-on-a-Stick configuration. Since all inter-VLAN traffic is routed through a single router interface, performance may be impacted if the router becomes a bottleneck or experiences high traffic loads. Additionally, Router-on-a-Stick configuration may not be suitable for large-scale deployments with high volumes of inter-VLAN traffic, as it may result in degraded network performance and increased latency.

In summary, Router-on-a-Stick configuration is a valuable technique for enabling routing between multiple VLANs using a single physical router interface. By configuring the router interface as a trunk port and creating subinterfaces for each VLAN, administrators can efficiently route traffic between VLANs without the need for dedicated router interfaces for each VLAN. This approach offers advantages in terms of cost-effectiveness, simplified network design, and flexibility in VLAN deployment, making it a valuable solution for small to medium-sized network environments.

Layer 3 switch Inter-VLAN routing setup is a crucial aspect of network design and management, allowing for efficient communication between different VLANs at Layer 3 of the OSI model. Unlike traditional Layer 2 switches that forward traffic based on MAC addresses, Layer 3 switches have the capability to route traffic based on IP addresses, making them ideal for inter-VLAN routing. By configuring a Layer 3 switch to perform inter-VLAN routing, network administrators can segment their networks into multiple virtual LANs (VLANs) while enabling communication between VLANs via the switch itself, eliminating the need for an external router.

To deploy Layer 3 switch Inter-VLAN routing, the first step is to configure the switch interfaces and VLANs accordingly. VLANs are logical segmentation of the network that allow administrators to group devices based on criteria such as department, location, or function. Using the command line interface (CLI), administrators can create VLANs on the Layer 3 switch and assign VLAN IDs to them. For example, on a Cisco Catalyst switch, the command to create a VLAN and assign an ID to it is:

arduinoCopy code

```
switch(config)# vlan <vlan-id>
```

Once the VLANs are created, the next step is to assign switch interfaces to the appropriate VLANs. This involves configuring switch ports as access ports and assigning them to specific VLANs. For example, to assign an interface to VLAN 10, the command would be:

arduinoCopy code

```
switch(config)# interface <interface> switch(config-if)# switchport mode access switch(config-if)# switchport access vlan 10
```

After configuring VLANs and assigning interfaces to them, the Layer 3 switch needs to be configured to perform routing between VLANs. This is achieved by enabling IP routing on the switch and configuring IP addresses for the VLAN interfaces. Each VLAN interface acts as a virtual router interface (SVI) for the corresponding VLAN, allowing the switch to route traffic between VLANs at Layer 3. The command to enable IP routing on a Layer 3 switch is:

arduinoCopy code

```
switch(config)# ip routing
```

Once IP routing is enabled, administrators can configure the IP addresses for the VLAN interfaces using the following commands:

arduinoCopy code

```
switch(config)# interface vlan <vlan-id> switch(config-if)# ip address <ip-address> <subnet-mask> switch(config-if)# no shutdown
```

For example, to configure the IP address 192.168.10.1/24 for VLAN 10, the commands would be:

arduinoCopy code

```
switch(config)# interface vlan 10 switch(config-if)# ip address 192.168.10.1 255.255.255.0 switch(config-if)# no shutdown
```

With Inter-VLAN routing configured on the Layer 3 switch, devices in different VLANs can communicate with each other using their respective IP addresses. When a device sends traffic to a device in another VLAN, the Layer 3 switch routes the traffic between the VLANs based on the destination IP address. This allows for efficient communication between devices in different VLANs without the need for an external router.

In addition to basic Inter-VLAN routing setup, administrators can implement advanced features such as access control lists (ACLs) and quality of service (QoS) policies to control and prioritize traffic between VLANs.

ACLs can be used to filter traffic based on source/destination IP addresses, protocols, or port numbers, providing security and traffic control at the network perimeter. QoS policies can be used to prioritize certain types of traffic, such as voice or video, over others to ensure optimal performance for critical applications.

Furthermore, administrators can implement routing protocols such as OSPF (Open Shortest Path First) or EIGRP (Enhanced Interior Gateway Routing Protocol) to dynamically exchange routing information between Layer 3 switches and external routers, allowing for scalable and resilient network designs. By deploying Layer 3 switch Inter-VLAN routing setup with advanced features and routing protocols, organizations can build robust and efficient network infrastructures that meet the demands of modern business applications and services.

In summary, Layer 3 switch Inter-VLAN routing setup is a fundamental aspect of network design, allowing for efficient communication between VLANs at Layer 3 of the OSI model. By configuring a Layer 3 switch to perform Inter-VLAN routing, administrators can segment their networks into multiple VLANs while enabling communication between VLANs via the switch itself, eliminating the need for an external router. With advanced features such as ACLs, QoS policies, and routing protocols, organizations can build scalable and resilient network infrastructures that meet their business requirements.

Chapter 4: High Availability and Redundancy in Switching

Redundant link configurations are essential elements in network design, providing fault tolerance and resilience by ensuring network connectivity even in the event of link failures or equipment malfunctions. Redundant links can be deployed at various levels of the network architecture, including access, distribution, and core layers, to minimize downtime and maintain network availability. By configuring redundant links, network administrators can improve network reliability and performance, ensuring uninterrupted access to critical resources and services.

At the access layer, redundant link configurations are typically implemented using techniques such as EtherChannel or Link Aggregation Control Protocol (LACP). EtherChannel allows multiple physical links between switches to be bundled together into a single logical link, increasing bandwidth and providing redundancy in case of link failures. To configure EtherChannel on Cisco Catalyst switches, administrators can use the following commands:

arduinoCopy code

```
switch(config)# interface range <interface-range>
switch(config-if-range)# channel-group <channel-group> mode <mode>
```

In this command, "<interface-range>" specifies the range of interfaces to be bundled into the EtherChannel, "<channel-group>" specifies the EtherChannel number, and "<mode>" specifies the EtherChannel mode (e.g., "active" for LACP or "on" for static EtherChannel).

Similarly, at the distribution and core layers, redundant link configurations are commonly implemented using protocols such as Spanning Tree Protocol (STP) or its variants such as Rapid Spanning Tree Protocol (RSTP) or Multiple Spanning Tree Protocol (MSTP). STP detects and blocks redundant links in the network topology to prevent loops and ensure a loop-free topology. RSTP and MSTP provide faster convergence and better scalability compared to traditional STP, making them suitable for modern network environments.

To configure STP on a Cisco Catalyst switch, administrators can use the following command:

arduinoCopy code

```
switch(config)# spanning-tree vlan <vlan-id> priority <priority-value>
```

This command sets the priority value for a specific VLAN, influencing the selection of the root bridge in the STP topology. Lower priority values indicate a higher priority for becoming the root bridge, allowing administrators to control the placement of the root bridge in the network topology.

In addition to Layer 2 redundancy, redundant link configurations can also be implemented at Layer 3 using routing protocols such as Hot Standby Router Protocol (HSRP), Virtual Router Redundancy Protocol (VRRP), or Gateway Load Balancing Protocol (GLBP). These protocols provide redundancy for default gateway services, allowing multiple routers to share a single virtual IP address and provide seamless failover in case of router failures.

To configure HSRP on Cisco routers, administrators can use the following commands:

arduinoCopy code

```
router(config)# interface <interface> router(config-if)# standby <group-number> ip <virtual-ip> router(config-if)# standby <group-number> priority <priority-value>
```

In this command, "<interface>" specifies the interface to be configured for HSRP, "<group-number>" specifies the HSRP group number, "<virtual-ip>" specifies the virtual IP address used by the HSRP group, and "<priority-value>" specifies the priority value for the router in the HSRP group. The router with the highest priority value becomes the active router for the HSRP group.

Furthermore, redundant link configurations can be enhanced with technologies such as Quality of Service (QoS) and load balancing to optimize network performance and resource utilization. QoS allows administrators to prioritize certain types of traffic over others, ensuring that critical applications receive sufficient bandwidth and latency requirements are met. Load balancing distributes traffic across redundant links to maximize bandwidth utilization and prevent link congestion, improving overall network efficiency.

To configure QoS on Cisco routers or switches, administrators can use the following commands: arduinoCopy code

```
switch(config)#          class-map          <class-name>
switch(config-cmap)#          match          <criteria>
switch(config)#          policy-map          <policy-name>
switch(config-pmap)#          class          <class-name>
switch(config-pmap-c)#     <action>     switch(config)#
interface     <interface>     switch(config-if)#     service-policy input <policy-name>
```

In this command sequence, "<class-name>" specifies the name of the traffic class, "<criteria>" specifies the criteria for matching traffic (e.g., access control lists or packet attributes), "<policy-name>" specifies the name of the QoS policy, and "<action>" specifies the action to be taken on matched traffic (e.g., prioritization or traffic shaping).

Overall, redundant link configurations play a critical role in network design, providing fault tolerance and resilience to ensure uninterrupted network connectivity and service availability. By leveraging techniques such as EtherChannel, STP, HSRP, and QoS, administrators can build robust and reliable network infrastructures that meet the demands of modern business environments. Through proper planning, deployment, and maintenance of redundant link configurations, organizations can minimize downtime, improve performance, and enhance the overall reliability of their network infrastructure.

Implementing high availability features in switches is crucial for ensuring uninterrupted network operation and minimizing downtime. High availability features enhance network resilience by providing redundancy and failover mechanisms, allowing switches to maintain continuous operation even in the event of hardware failures or network disruptions. By deploying high availability features, such as redundant power supplies, hot-swappable components, and protocols like Virtual Router Redundancy Protocol (VRRP) or Hot Standby Router Protocol (HSRP), organizations can improve network reliability and minimize the impact of potential failures.

One of the fundamental high availability features in switches is the deployment of redundant power supplies. Redundant power supplies ensure that switches remain powered even if one power supply unit fails. Most enterprise-grade switches support the installation of multiple power supply units, allowing administrators to configure them in a redundant configuration. In the event of a power supply failure, the backup power supply unit automatically takes over, ensuring continuous operation without interruption. To configure redundant power supplies on a switch, administrators can install the additional power supply units and use the switch's CLI to enable redundancy and monitor power supply status.

Another important aspect of high availability in switches is the use of hot-swappable components, such as fan modules and interface cards. Hot-swappable components can be replaced or upgraded without disrupting switch operation, allowing administrators to perform maintenance tasks or replace faulty components without causing downtime. Most modern switches support hot-swappable components, enabling administrators to perform replacements or upgrades while the switch remains operational. To replace a hot-swappable component, administrators can use the appropriate CLI commands to identify the faulty component, remove it from the switch chassis, and insert the replacement component.

In addition to hardware redundancy, high availability in switches can be achieved through the implementation of redundancy protocols such as Virtual Router Redundancy Protocol (VRRP) or Hot Standby Router Protocol (HSRP). These protocols enable multiple switches to share a virtual IP address and provide redundant gateway services to connected devices. In the event of a switch failure, the backup switch automatically assumes the role of the active gateway, ensuring uninterrupted connectivity for network devices. To configure redundancy protocols on switches, administrators can use the CLI to define virtual router groups, assign IP addresses, and specify priority settings to determine the active and standby switches.

Furthermore, high availability features in switches can include mechanisms for detecting and mitigating network disruptions, such as link failures or network congestion. Rapid Spanning Tree Protocol (RSTP) and its variants, such as Multiple Spanning Tree Protocol (MSTP), provide fast convergence and loop prevention in redundant network topologies, reducing the impact of link failures and ensuring optimal network performance. Additionally, Quality of Service (QoS) mechanisms can be deployed to prioritize critical traffic and ensure that bandwidth is allocated appropriately during network congestion. To configure RSTP or MSTP on switches, administrators can use the CLI to enable the protocols and configure parameters such as bridge priority and port costs.

Moreover, switches with advanced high availability features may support features such as stateful failover and non-stop forwarding, which allow for seamless failover and uninterrupted packet forwarding in the event of switch or network failures. Stateful failover ensures that session information and packet forwarding state are synchronized between redundant switches, minimizing disruption for active network connections. Non-stop forwarding enables switches to continue forwarding traffic even during software upgrades or system reboots, ensuring continuous operation without interruption. To configure stateful failover or non-stop forwarding on switches, administrators can use the CLI to enable the appropriate features and configure synchronization settings.

Overall, implementing high availability features in switches is essential for ensuring reliable and resilient network operation. By deploying redundant power supplies, hot-swappable components, redundancy protocols, and mechanisms for detecting and mitigating network disruptions, organizations can minimize downtime and maintain continuous connectivity for critical network services. Through proper planning, configuration, and maintenance of high availability features, administrators can build robust and resilient network infrastructures that meet the demands of modern business environments.

Chapter 5: Quality of Service (QoS) in Switched Networks

Quality of Service (QoS) principles and objectives are fundamental aspects of network design and management, aimed at ensuring optimal performance and resource utilization for critical applications and services. QoS encompasses a set of techniques and mechanisms that prioritize and control network traffic based on predefined criteria, such as application type, traffic characteristics, or user requirements. The primary objectives of QoS implementation are to guarantee bandwidth, minimize latency, reduce packet loss, and ensure predictable performance for specific types of traffic, thereby enhancing overall network efficiency and user experience.

To achieve the objectives of QoS, network administrators can deploy various QoS mechanisms and techniques, including traffic classification, congestion management, congestion avoidance, and traffic shaping. Traffic classification involves identifying and categorizing network traffic into different classes or priority levels based on specific criteria, such as application type, source/destination IP address, or Layer 4 port number. By classifying traffic, administrators can apply different QoS policies and treatment to each traffic class, ensuring that critical applications receive preferential treatment over less important traffic.

One of the key QoS mechanisms for achieving bandwidth guarantees and minimizing latency is congestion management, which involves the use of queuing algorithms to prioritize and schedule packet transmission during periods of network congestion. Popular queuing algorithms include First-In-First-Out (FIFO), Priority Queuing (PQ), Weighted Fair Queuing (WFQ), and Class-Based Queuing (CBQ). Administrators can configure queuing mechanisms on network devices using the appropriate CLI commands to specify queue types, thresholds, and scheduling parameters based on the specific requirements of the network and applications.

Congestion avoidance is another important QoS mechanism aimed at preventing network congestion before it occurs by dynamically adjusting packet transmission rates based on network conditions. One commonly used congestion avoidance mechanism is Random Early Detection (RED), which monitors packet queue lengths and selectively drops packets before the queue becomes congested. By dropping packets proactively, RED helps to regulate traffic flow and prevent packet loss during periods of congestion, thereby improving overall network performance and stability.

In addition to congestion management and avoidance, traffic shaping is a QoS technique used to control the rate of traffic transmission to ensure that it conforms to predefined traffic profiles or service level agreements (SLAs). Traffic shaping allows administrators to limit the bandwidth usage of certain types of traffic, shape traffic bursts, and smooth out traffic flows to prevent congestion and optimize network performance. To configure traffic shaping on network devices, administrators can use CLI commands to specify traffic shaping policies, bandwidth limits, and traffic shaping parameters.

Furthermore, QoS mechanisms can be applied at various network layers, including Layer 2 (Data Link Layer) and Layer 3 (Network Layer), to prioritize and control traffic based on different criteria. At Layer 2, administrators can implement QoS features such as IEEE 802.1p priority tagging and Differentiated Services Code Point (DSCP) marking to prioritize traffic at the Ethernet frame level. At Layer 3, protocols such as IP precedence and Differentiated Services (DiffServ) can be used to classify and mark packets with different priority levels based on their IP headers.

Moreover, QoS principles can be applied across different types of network technologies and environments, including local area networks (LANs), wide area networks (WANs), and wireless networks. In LAN environments, QoS mechanisms can be deployed to prioritize traffic between devices within the same network segment, ensuring that critical applications receive sufficient bandwidth and low latency. In WAN environments, QoS techniques such as Traffic Engineering (TE) and Multiprotocol Label Switching (MPLS) can be used to optimize traffic routing and resource allocation across distributed network infrastructure.

In wireless networks, QoS mechanisms play a critical role in ensuring reliable and efficient communication between wireless devices and access points. Techniques such as Wi-Fi Multimedia (WMM) and Wireless Multimedia Extensions (WME) provide QoS support for wireless traffic, allowing administrators to prioritize voice, video, and data traffic based on application requirements and network conditions. By implementing QoS in wireless networks, organizations can improve the performance and reliability of wireless communication and support a wide range of applications and services.

Overall, QoS principles and objectives are essential for optimizing network performance, ensuring efficient resource utilization, and delivering a consistent and reliable user experience. By deploying QoS mechanisms and techniques, administrators can prioritize critical traffic, mitigate congestion, and guarantee quality of service for specific applications and services, thereby enhancing overall network efficiency and user satisfaction. Through proper planning, configuration, and monitoring of QoS policies, organizations can build robust and scalable network infrastructures that meet the demands of modern business environments.

Configuring Quality of Service (QoS) policies for switched networks is essential for optimizing network performance and ensuring efficient resource utilization. QoS policies allow network administrators to prioritize critical traffic, mitigate congestion, and guarantee quality of service for specific applications and services. By deploying QoS policies on switches, administrators can control and manage traffic flows based on predefined criteria, such as application type, traffic characteristics, or user requirements.

One of the first steps in configuring QoS policies for switched networks is to define traffic classification criteria. Traffic classification involves identifying and categorizing network traffic into different classes or priority levels based on specific criteria. Administrators can use various classification methods, such as access control lists (ACLs), IP precedence, Differentiated Services Code Point (DSCP), or Layer 4 port numbers, to classify traffic flows. For example, to classify traffic based on IP precedence, administrators can use the "ip precedence" command in Cisco IOS to set the IP precedence value for specific traffic:

arduinoCopy code

```
switch(config)# access-list <access-list-number> permit <protocol> <source> <destination>
switch(config)# class-map <class-map-name>
switch(config-cmap)# match access-group <access-list-number>
switch(config)# policy-map <policy-
```

map-name> switch(config-pmap)# class <class-map-name> switch(config-pmap-c)# set ip precedence <precedence-value>

In this example, "<access-list-number>" specifies the ACL number, "<protocol>" specifies the protocol type, "<source>" and "<destination>" specify the source and destination IP addresses, "<class-map-name>" specifies the name of the class map, and "<precedence-value>" specifies the IP precedence value to be set for the matched traffic.

Once traffic classification criteria are defined, administrators can proceed to configure QoS policies for traffic prioritization and treatment. QoS policies typically consist of traffic classes, traffic marking, and traffic policing or shaping. Traffic classes define the different types of traffic flows and their corresponding QoS treatment, while traffic marking involves setting QoS markings such as IP precedence, DSCP, or class of service (CoS) values to indicate the priority level of traffic. Traffic policing or shaping mechanisms control the rate of traffic transmission to ensure that it conforms to predefined traffic profiles or service level agreements (SLAs).

To configure QoS policies for traffic prioritization on switches, administrators can use the following CLI commands to define class maps, policy maps, and apply QoS policies to switch interfaces:

arduinoCopy code

```
switch(config)#      class-map      <class-map-name>
switch(config-cmap)#         match         <criteria>
switch(config)#    policy-map    <policy-map-name>
switch(config-pmap)#     class     <class-map-name>
switch(config-pmap-c)#    <action>    switch(config)#
interface    <interface>    switch(config-if)#    service-
policy input <policy-map-name>
```

In this command sequence, "<class-map-name>" specifies the name of the class map, "<criteria>" specifies the criteria for matching traffic (e.g., ACLs, IP precedence, DSCP), "<policy-map-name>" specifies the name of the policy map, and "<action>" specifies the action to be taken on matched traffic (e.g., prioritization, traffic shaping). Administrators can apply the QoS policy to switch interfaces using the "service-policy input" command.

Furthermore, administrators can configure QoS policies to provide different levels of QoS treatment for various types of traffic. For example, administrators can prioritize voice and video traffic over data traffic to ensure low latency and minimal packet loss for real-time applications. To achieve this, administrators can define separate traffic classes for voice, video, and data traffic and apply different QoS policies to each class to prioritize traffic accordingly.

Additionally, administrators can monitor and troubleshoot QoS configurations on switches to ensure that QoS policies are effectively applied and traffic is being prioritized as intended. CLI commands such as "show policy-map interface" can be used to display statistics and information about QoS policies applied to switch interfaces, allowing administrators to verify QoS configurations and identify any potential issues or bottlenecks in the network.

Overall, configuring QoS policies for switched networks is a critical aspect of network management, enabling administrators to optimize network performance, prioritize critical traffic, and ensure quality of service for specific applications and services. By defining traffic classification criteria, configuring QoS policies for traffic prioritization, and monitoring QoS configurations, administrators can effectively manage network resources and deliver a consistent and reliable user experience across the network.

Chapter 6: Port Security and Access Control Lists (ACLs)

Port security measures and configuration are essential components of network security, aimed at preventing unauthorized access to network resources and protecting against potential security threats. Port security involves implementing policies and mechanisms to control access to switch ports, monitor and restrict the number of devices connected to a port, and mitigate risks associated with unauthorized access or malicious activities. By configuring port security measures on switches, network administrators can enhance the overall security posture of the network and safeguard against unauthorized access and potential security breaches.

One of the fundamental port security measures is port lockdown, which involves configuring switch ports to restrict access to authorized devices only. Administrators can use the port security feature available on most enterprise-grade switches to specify the maximum number of MAC addresses allowed on a port and dynamically learn and secure the MAC addresses of connected devices. To configure port security on a switch port, administrators can use the following CLI commands:

arduinoCopy code

switch(config)# interface <interface> switch(config-if)# switchport mode access switch(config-if)# switchport port-security switch(config-if)# switchport

port-security maximum <max-mac-addresses> switch(config-if)# switchport port-security violation <violation-mode> switch(config-if)# switchport port-security mac-address <mac-address>

In this command sequence, "<interface>" specifies the switch port interface to be configured, and "<max-mac-addresses>" specifies the maximum number of MAC addresses allowed on the port. Administrators can specify the violation mode ("<violation-mode>") to determine the action taken when a violation occurs, such as shutting down the port, generating a syslog message, or forwarding traffic while logging the violation. Additionally, administrators can manually configure authorized MAC addresses ("<mac-address>") on the port to restrict access to specific devices.

Another important port security measure is MAC address lockdown, which involves statically configuring MAC addresses on switch ports to restrict access to specific devices. MAC address lockdown prevents unauthorized devices from connecting to the network by allowing only preconfigured MAC addresses to communicate through the switch port. To configure MAC address lockdown on a switch port, administrators can use the following CLI commands:

arduinoCopy code

switch(config)# interface <interface> switch(config-if)# switchport mode access switch(config-if)# switchport port-security switch(config-if)# switchport port-security maximum 1 switch(config-if)# switchport port-security violation <violation-mode> switch(config-if)# switchport port-security mac-address <mac-address>

In this command sequence, administrators configure the port in access mode ("<switchport mode access>") and enable port security ("<switchport port-security>"). The maximum number of MAC addresses allowed on the port is set to one ("<switchport port-security maximum 1>"), effectively implementing MAC address lockdown. Administrators can specify the violation mode and manually configure the authorized MAC address ("<mac-address>") on the port.

Additionally, administrators can leverage additional port security features, such as sticky MAC address learning and aging, to enhance port security measures. Sticky MAC address learning allows the switch to dynamically learn the MAC addresses of devices connected to the port and automatically configure them as authorized MAC addresses. Administrators can enable sticky MAC address learning on a switch port using the following CLI command:

arduinoCopy code

switch(config-if)# switchport port-security mac-address sticky

By enabling sticky MAC address learning, administrators can streamline the configuration process and ensure that only authorized devices are allowed to access the network through the port. Furthermore, administrators can configure MAC address aging to remove dynamically learned MAC addresses from the port's secure MAC address table after a specified period of inactivity, helping to maintain port security and prevent unauthorized access.

Overall, port security measures and configuration play a crucial role in safeguarding network resources and mitigating security risks associated with unauthorized access. By implementing port security features such as port lockdown, MAC address lockdown, sticky MAC address learning, and MAC address aging, administrators can control access to switch ports, monitor and restrict the number of devices connected to the network, and protect against potential security threats and malicious activities. Through proper planning, configuration, and monitoring of port security measures, organizations can strengthen the overall security posture of their networks and ensure the integrity and confidentiality of sensitive information.

Access Control Lists (ACLs) are essential components of network security, providing a means to control and filter traffic based on defined criteria. ACL implementation for traffic filtering is a fundamental aspect of network administration, allowing administrators to define policies that permit or deny traffic flows based on various parameters, such as source and destination IP addresses, protocols, ports, and packet characteristics. By deploying ACLs on routers and switches, administrators can enforce security policies, mitigate risks associated with unauthorized access, and protect network resources from malicious activities.

One of the primary use cases for ACLs is to restrict access to network resources by blocking traffic from unauthorized sources. Administrators can use ACLs to define rules that explicitly deny traffic from specific IP addresses, IP ranges, or subnets, thereby preventing unauthorized users or devices from accessing sensitive network resources. To implement ACLs for traffic filtering on Cisco routers, administrators can use the following CLI commands:

arduinoCopy code

```
router(config)# access-list <acl-number> {permit | deny} <protocol> <source> <destination> [eq | gt | lt] <port> router(config)# interface <interface> router(config-if)# ip access-group <acl-number> {in | out}
```

In this command sequence, "<acl-number>" specifies the ACL number, "<protocol>" specifies the protocol type (e.g., TCP, UDP, ICMP), "<source>" and "<destination>" specify the source and destination IP addresses or networks, and "<port>" specifies the port number or range. Administrators can choose whether to permit or deny traffic matching the ACL criteria. The ACL is then applied to the inbound or outbound direction of the specified interface ("<interface>") using the "ip access-group" command.

Additionally, ACLs can be used to filter traffic based on specific application-layer protocols or services. For example, administrators can create ACL rules to permit or deny traffic for specific services such as HTTP, FTP, SSH, or DNS. By filtering traffic at the application layer, administrators can enforce security policies tailored to the requirements of specific applications and services. To implement ACLs for filtering traffic based on application-layer protocols, administrators can use extended ACLs and specify the protocol type and port numbers in the ACL rules:

arduinoCopy code

```
router(config)# access-list <acl-number> {permit | deny} <protocol> <source> <destination> [eq | gt | lt] <port>
```

In this command, "<protocol>" specifies the application-layer protocol (e.g., TCP, UDP), and "<port>" specifies the port number or range associated with the protocol. Administrators can create ACL rules to permit or deny traffic for specific application-layer protocols based on their requirements.

Moreover, ACLs can be used to filter traffic based on packet characteristics such as packet size, Time-to-Live (TTL) values, or IP options. Administrators can create ACL rules to permit or deny traffic based on packet attributes, helping to prevent certain types of network attacks or anomalies. To implement ACLs for filtering traffic based on packet characteristics, administrators can use extended ACLs and specify the desired packet attributes in the ACL rules:

arduinoCopy code

```
router(config)# access-list <acl-number> {permit | deny} <protocol> <source> <destination> [options]
```

In this command, "<protocol>" specifies the protocol type (e.g., IP), and "[options]" specify additional packet attributes such as packet size or TTL values. Administrators can create ACL rules to permit or deny traffic based on specific packet characteristics to enhance network security and protect against potential threats.

Furthermore, ACLs can be deployed in conjunction with other security features such as Virtual Private Networks (VPNs), firewalls, and Intrusion Detection Systems (IDS) to provide comprehensive network security and threat mitigation. By integrating ACLs with these security technologies, administrators can create layered defenses that protect against a wide range of security threats and vulnerabilities. Additionally, administrators can regularly review and update ACL configurations to adapt to changing network requirements and emerging security threats, ensuring that ACLs remain effective in enforcing security policies and protecting network resources.

Overall, ACL implementation for traffic filtering is a critical aspect of network security, enabling administrators to control and restrict traffic flows based on defined criteria. By deploying ACLs on routers and switches, administrators can enforce security policies, mitigate risks associated with unauthorized access, and protect network resources from malicious activities. Through proper planning, configuration, and monitoring of ACLs, organizations can strengthen the overall security posture of their networks and ensure the integrity and confidentiality of sensitive information.

Chapter 7: EtherChannel Configuration and Load Balancing

EtherChannel, also known as link aggregation or port-channel, is a technique used in networking to combine multiple physical links into a single logical link, providing increased bandwidth, redundancy, and load balancing capabilities. EtherChannel allows multiple parallel links between switches or routers to be aggregated into a single logical interface, effectively increasing the bandwidth and enhancing the resiliency of network connections. This technique is commonly deployed in environments where high availability and improved performance are critical requirements.

The configuration of EtherChannel involves several steps to create and configure the logical bundle of physical links. The first step is to select the physical interfaces that will be part of the EtherChannel bundle. Administrators can choose multiple physical interfaces and group them together to form the EtherChannel. To configure EtherChannel on Cisco switches, administrators can use the following CLI command:

arduinoCopy code

switch(config)# interface range <interface-range>
switch(config-if-range)# channel-group <channel-group-number> mode <mode>

In this command, "<interface-range>" specifies the range of physical interfaces to be included in the EtherChannel bundle, and "<channel-group-number>"

specifies the number of the EtherChannel interface. The "mode" parameter specifies the EtherChannel negotiation mode, which can be set to "on" for static EtherChannel configuration or "auto" or "desirable" for dynamic negotiation using protocols such as Port Aggregation Protocol (PAgP) or Link Aggregation Control Protocol (LACP).

After configuring the physical interfaces and assigning them to the EtherChannel bundle, administrators need to configure the EtherChannel interface itself. This involves creating a logical interface for the EtherChannel bundle and configuring any additional settings or parameters. To configure the EtherChannel interface, administrators can use the following CLI command:

arduinoCopy code

switch (config)# interface port-channel <channel-group-number> switch (config-if)# <additional-configuration>

In this command, "<channel-group-number>" specifies the number of the EtherChannel interface created earlier. Administrators can then configure additional settings for the EtherChannel interface, such as IP address, VLAN assignment, or any other parameters required for the specific network configuration.

Once the EtherChannel interface is configured, administrators can verify the status and operation of the EtherChannel bundle using various monitoring and troubleshooting commands. One common command used to verify the status of EtherChannel interfaces is the "show etherchannel summary" command, which displays information about the EtherChannel bundle, including the status of individual member interfaces and the overall status of the bundle. Administrators can use this command to ensure that the EtherChannel bundle is operational and that all member interfaces are functioning correctly.

In addition to basic configuration and monitoring, administrators can also fine-tune the behavior and characteristics of EtherChannel bundles using advanced configuration options. For example, administrators can configure load balancing algorithms to distribute traffic across member interfaces based on specific criteria such as source and destination MAC addresses, IP addresses, or TCP/UDP port numbers. By configuring load balancing, administrators can optimize the utilization of available bandwidth and improve the performance of the network.

Another important consideration when configuring EtherChannel is the choice of negotiation protocol. EtherChannel supports both static configuration and dynamic negotiation using protocols such as PAgP and LACP. Static EtherChannel configuration involves manually configuring the bundle without negotiation, while dynamic negotiation protocols allow switches to automatically negotiate the formation of EtherChannel bundles based on predefined criteria. Administrators can choose the appropriate negotiation protocol based on their specific requirements and compatibility with existing network infrastructure.

Overall, EtherChannel provides a flexible and efficient solution for aggregating multiple physical links into a single logical interface, offering increased bandwidth, redundancy, and load balancing capabilities. By following the configuration steps outlined above and leveraging advanced features and options, administrators can deploy EtherChannel effectively in their networks to improve performance, reliability, and scalability.

Load balancing techniques in EtherChannel setup play a crucial role in optimizing network performance and resource utilization by distributing traffic evenly across multiple physical links within the EtherChannel bundle. EtherChannel, also known as link aggregation, enables the bundling of multiple physical links into a single logical interface, providing increased bandwidth and redundancy. Load balancing ensures that network traffic is efficiently distributed across these links, preventing congestion and maximizing the utilization of available resources. There are various load balancing algorithms and techniques available for EtherChannel configuration, each offering unique advantages and suitability for different network environments.

One commonly used load balancing technique in EtherChannel setup is based on source and destination MAC addresses. This technique, often referred to as MAC address-based load balancing, distributes traffic across member links based on the source and destination MAC addresses of incoming packets. By examining the MAC addresses, switches can determine which link to use for forwarding traffic, ensuring that traffic between specific source and destination pairs is evenly distributed across the available links. To configure MAC address-based load balancing on an EtherChannel bundle, administrators can use the following CLI command:

arduinoCopy code

switch(config)# port-channel load-balance src-dst-mac

In this command, "port-channel load-balance src-dst-mac" specifies the load balancing algorithm based on source and destination MAC addresses.

Another commonly used load balancing technique is based on source and destination IP addresses. This technique, known as IP address-based load balancing, distributes traffic across member links based on the source and destination IP addresses of incoming packets. By analyzing the IP addresses, switches can determine the appropriate link for forwarding traffic, ensuring that traffic between different IP address pairs is evenly distributed across the available links. To configure IP address-based load balancing on an EtherChannel bundle, administrators can use the following CLI command:

arduinoCopy code

switch(config)# port-channel load-balance src-dst-ip

In this command, "port-channel load-balance src-dst-ip" specifies the load balancing algorithm based on source and destination IP addresses.

Additionally, EtherChannel supports load balancing based on TCP and UDP port numbers. This technique, often referred to as port-based load balancing, distributes traffic across member links based on the TCP or UDP port numbers of incoming packets. By examining the port numbers, switches can determine which link to use for forwarding traffic, ensuring that traffic for different applications or services is evenly distributed across the available links. To configure port-based load balancing on an EtherChannel bundle, administrators can use the following CLI command:

arduinoCopy code

switch(config)# port-channel load-balance src-dst-port

In this command, "port-channel load-balance src-dst-port" specifies the load balancing algorithm based on source and destination port numbers.

Moreover, EtherChannel supports a combination of load balancing techniques, allowing administrators to customize the load balancing behavior based on specific criteria or network requirements. For example, administrators can configure EtherChannel to use a combination of MAC address-based and IP address-based load balancing to achieve optimal traffic distribution across member links. To configure a combination of load balancing techniques on an EtherChannel bundle, administrators can use the following CLI command:

arduinoCopy code

switch(config)# port-channel load-balance <method1> <method2>

In this command, "<method1>" and "<method2>" specify the load balancing algorithms to be used in combination, such as src-dst-mac, src-dst-ip, or src-dst-port.

Furthermore, administrators can monitor and verify the effectiveness of load balancing techniques using various CLI commands and monitoring tools. For example, the "show etherchannel load-balance" command allows administrators to view the current load balancing configuration and verify which algorithm is being used for traffic distribution. Additionally, network monitoring tools can provide real-time insights into traffic patterns and link utilization, helping administrators identify potential bottlenecks or performance issues and adjust load balancing configurations accordingly.

Overall, load balancing techniques in EtherChannel setup are essential for optimizing network performance, enhancing resource utilization, and ensuring high availability. By configuring load balancing algorithms based on source and destination MAC addresses, IP addresses, or port numbers, administrators can distribute traffic evenly across member links within an EtherChannel bundle, preventing congestion and maximizing the efficiency of network resources. Through proper configuration, monitoring, and adjustment of load balancing techniques, organizations can achieve optimal performance and reliability in their network environments.

Chapter 8: Advanced Switching Technologies: VTP, PVST, and Rapid STP

VTP (VLAN Trunking Protocol) configuration is a fundamental aspect of managing VLANs (Virtual Local Area Networks) in Cisco networking environments, providing a convenient way to propagate VLAN information across switches in a network. VTP simplifies VLAN management by allowing administrators to create, modify, and delete VLANs on a single switch and have those changes automatically propagated to other switches in the same VTP domain. This centralized approach streamlines VLAN administration and ensures consistency across the network, reducing the likelihood of misconfigurations and inconsistencies.

To configure VTP on Cisco switches, administrators must first define a VTP domain name, which is a logical grouping of switches that share VLAN information. Each switch in a VTP domain must have the same domain name to participate in VTP updates. The VTP domain name can be configured using the following CLI command:

arduinoCopy code

switch(config)# vtp domain <domain-name>

In this command, "<domain-name>" specifies the name of the VTP domain.

After configuring the VTP domain name, administrators must configure the VTP mode for each switch. VTP supports three modes: server, client, and transparent. The server mode allows switches to create, modify, and delete VLANs and propagate VTP advertisements to other switches in the domain. The client mode allows switches to receive VTP advertisements and update their VLAN configurations accordingly, but they cannot create or modify VLANs. The transparent mode forwards VTP advertisements but does not participate in VTP updates, allowing switches to maintain their VLAN configurations independently. Administrators can configure the VTP mode using the following CLI command:

arduinoCopy code

```
switch(config)# vtp mode {server | client | transparent}
```

In this command, "{server | client | transparent}" specifies the desired VTP mode.

Additionally, administrators can configure VTP version and password settings to enhance security and compatibility. VTP version determines the format of VTP advertisements and the features supported by VTP. By default, Cisco switches use VTP version 1, but administrators can configure switches to use VTP version 2 for enhanced features and security. The VTP password, also known as the domain password, is a shared secret used to authenticate VTP advertisements between switches in the same domain. To configure VTP version and password settings, administrators can use the following CLI commands:

arduinoCopy code

```
switch(config)# vtp version {1 | 2}  switch(config)# vtp password <password>
```

In these commands, "{1 | 2}" specifies the desired VTP version, and "<password>" specifies the VTP domain password.

Furthermore, administrators can configure VLANs on VTP server switches and have those VLAN configurations automatically propagated to other switches in the same domain. VLAN creation and modification are performed in VLAN configuration mode using the following CLI command:

arduinoCopy code

```
switch(config)# vlan <vlan-id>
```

In this command, "<vlan-id>" specifies the VLAN identifier.

Once VTP is configured on switches within a VTP domain, administrators can monitor and verify the VTP status and operation using various CLI commands. For example, the "show vtp status" command provides information about the VTP domain name, mode, version, and password settings, as well as the status of VTP advertisements and synchronization. Additionally, the "show vlan" command displays information about VLANs configured on the switch, including VLAN IDs, names, and associated ports.

In summary, VTP configuration is essential for managing VLANs in Cisco networking environments, providing a centralized and efficient way to propagate VLAN information across switches. By configuring VTP domain names, modes, versions, and passwords, administrators can establish a consistent VLAN configuration across the network and streamline VLAN administration. Through proper configuration and monitoring of VTP, organizations can maintain VLAN consistency, improve network management efficiency, and reduce the risk of configuration errors.

PVST (Per-VLAN Spanning Tree) and Rapid STP (Spanning Tree Protocol) implementation are essential aspects of network design and configuration, particularly in environments where VLANs are deployed. Spanning Tree Protocol is a crucial mechanism used to prevent loops in Ethernet networks by selectively blocking redundant paths while keeping the network loop-free. PVST extends the functionality of STP by running a separate instance of STP for each VLAN, allowing for more efficient use of network resources and better network convergence times. Rapid STP, also known as RSTP or IEEE 802.1w, improves the convergence time of the spanning tree by significantly reducing the time it takes for the network to transition to a stable state after topology changes occur.

To implement PVST on Cisco switches, administrators must first enable STP globally on the switch. This can be achieved using the following CLI command:

arduinoCopy code

```
switch(config)# spanning-tree mode pvst
```

In this command, "spanning-tree mode pvst" configures the switch to operate in PVST mode, allowing for the creation of separate spanning tree instances for each VLAN.

After enabling PVST mode, administrators can configure additional parameters for each VLAN, such as the priority of the root bridge, to influence the spanning tree topology. The root bridge is the central switch in the spanning tree topology, and configuring its priority ensures that it becomes the root bridge for the VLAN. To configure the priority of the root bridge for a specific VLAN, administrators can use the following CLI command:

arduinoCopy code

```
switch(config)# spanning-tree vlan <vlan-id> root primary
```

In this command, "<vlan-id>" specifies the VLAN identifier, and "root primary" configures the switch to become the root bridge for the specified VLAN.

Furthermore, administrators can enable Rapid STP to improve the convergence time of the spanning tree and reduce the network downtime caused by topology changes. Rapid STP provides faster convergence by introducing new port roles and states, such as discarding and learning, to speed up the process of transitioning ports to forwarding mode. To enable Rapid STP on Cisco switches, administrators can use the following CLI command:

arduinoCopy code

switch(config)# spanning-tree mode rapid-pvst

In this command, "spanning-tree mode rapid-pvst" configures the switch to operate in Rapid PVST mode, enabling Rapid STP for faster convergence.

Additionally, administrators can configure portfast and bpduguard on access ports to enhance the stability and security of the network. Portfast allows access ports to transition directly to the forwarding state without going through the listening and learning states, reducing the time it takes for end devices to connect to the network. Bpduguard detects and disables ports that receive Bridge Protocol Data Units (BPDUs), which are indicators of potential loop configurations or unauthorized switches connected to the network. To enable portfast and bpduguard on access ports, administrators can use the following CLI commands:

arduinoCopy code

switch(config)#   interface   <interface-id>
switch(config-if)#   spanning-tree   portfast
switch(config-if)# spanning-tree bpduguard enable

In these commands, "<interface-id>" specifies the interface to be configured, such as a FastEthernet or GigabitEthernet interface.

Moreover, administrators can monitor and verify the spanning tree status and operation using various CLI commands and monitoring tools. For example, the "show spanning-tree" command provides information about the spanning tree topology, including the root bridge, port roles, and port states for each VLAN. Additionally, network monitoring tools can provide real-time insights into spanning tree changes and convergence times, allowing administrators to troubleshoot and optimize the network as needed.

In summary, PVST and Rapid STP implementation are essential for ensuring network stability, efficiency, and resilience in VLAN environments. By configuring switches to operate in PVST mode and enabling Rapid STP, administrators can create a loop-free topology with fast convergence times, reducing network downtime and improving overall reliability. Through proper configuration and monitoring of PVST and Rapid STP, organizations can maintain a robust and responsive network infrastructure capable of supporting critical business operations and applications.

Chapter 9: Multilayer Switching and Layer 3 Switching

Multilayer switching, also known as layer 3 switching, offers significant benefits for modern network architectures by combining the functionality of layer 2 switching with layer 3 routing. This integration allows switches to make forwarding decisions based on both MAC addresses and IP addresses, resulting in improved network performance, scalability, and efficiency. Multilayer switching offers several key advantages over traditional layer 2 switching, including faster packet forwarding, reduced network congestion, enhanced security, and simplified network management.

To configure multilayer switching on Cisco switches, administrators must first ensure that the switch supports layer 3 functionality. This typically involves using switches from the Cisco Catalyst series that offer multilayer switching capabilities. Once the hardware support is confirmed, administrators can configure layer 3 functionality on the switch by enabling IP routing using the following CLI command:

arduinoCopy code

switch(config)# ip routing

In this command, "ip routing" enables layer 3 IP routing on the switch, allowing it to make routing decisions based on IP addresses.

After enabling IP routing, administrators can configure layer 3 interfaces on the switch to facilitate routing between different network segments or VLANs. Layer 3 interfaces are typically configured on switch virtual interfaces (SVIs) for VLANs or on physical interfaces for routed ports. To configure a layer 3 interface for a VLAN using an SVI, administrators can use the following CLI commands:

arduinoCopy code

switch(config)# interface vlan <vlan-id> switch(config-if)# ip address <ip-address> <subnet-mask> switch(config-if)# no shutdown

In these commands, "<vlan-id>" specifies the VLAN identifier, "<ip-address>" specifies the IP address assigned to the interface, and "<subnet-mask>" specifies the subnet mask for the IP address. The "no shutdown" command enables the interface.

Alternatively, administrators can configure layer 3 interfaces on physical ports to create routed ports, allowing for direct routing between different network segments without the need for VLANs. To configure a routed port on a physical interface, administrators can use the following CLI commands:

arduinoCopy code

switch(config)# interface <interface-id> switch(config-if)# no switchport switch(config-if)# ip address <ip-address> <subnet-mask> switch(config-if)# no shutdown

In these commands, "<interface-id>" specifies the physical interface, "<ip-address>" specifies the IP address assigned to the interface, and "<subnet-mask>" specifies the subnet mask for the IP address. The "no switchport" command removes the layer 2 switching functionality from the interface, converting it into a layer 3 routed port.

Once layer 3 interfaces are configured, administrators can define routing protocols to facilitate dynamic routing between network segments. Common routing protocols used in multilayer switching environments include Routing Information Protocol (RIP), Enhanced Interior Gateway Routing Protocol (EIGRP), and Open Shortest Path First (OSPF). To configure a routing protocol on the switch, administrators can use the following CLI commands:

arduinoCopy code

```
switch(config)#           router           <routing-protocol>
switch(config-router)#    network    <network-address>
<wildcard-mask>
```

In these commands, "<routing-protocol>" specifies the routing protocol to be configured, and "<network-address>" and "<wildcard-mask>" specify the network address and wildcard mask for the network segment connected to the switch.

Moreover, administrators can implement advanced features such as access control lists (ACLs) and quality of service (QoS) policies to enhance security and prioritize network traffic in multilayer switching environments. ACLs can be used to filter traffic based on source or destination IP addresses, protocol types, or other criteria, while QoS policies can be used to prioritize certain types of traffic, such as voice or video traffic, over others. To configure ACLs and QoS policies on the switch, administrators can use the following CLI commands:

```
arduinoCopy code
switch(config)# access-list <acl-number> {permit |
deny} <protocol> <source> <destination>
switch(config)# interface <interface-id> switch(config-
if)# ip access-group <acl-number> <in | out>
switch(config)# class-map <class-map-name>
switch(config-cmap)# match <criteria> switch(config)#
policy-map <policy-map-name> switch(config-pmap)#
class <class-map-name> switch(config-pmap-c)#
{police | bandwidth} <value> switch(config)# interface
<interface-id> switch(config-if)# service-policy <input
| output> <policy-map-name>
```

In these commands, "<acl-number>" specifies the ACL number, "<protocol>" specifies the protocol type, "<source>" and "<destination>" specify the source and destination IP addresses, "<interface-id>" specifies the interface to which the ACL or QoS policy is applied, "<class-map-name>" specifies the name of the class map, and "<policy-map-name>" specifies the name of the policy map.

Additionally, administrators can monitor and verify the configuration and operation of multilayer switching using various CLI commands and monitoring tools. For example, the "show ip route" command displays the routing table on the switch, showing the routes learned through dynamic routing protocols or configured statically. The "show interface" command provides information about layer 3 interfaces, including their IP addresses, status, and packet statistics. Furthermore, network monitoring tools can provide real-time insights into traffic patterns, routing updates, and interface utilization, helping administrators troubleshoot and optimize the performance of multilayer switching environments.

In summary, multilayer switching offers significant benefits for modern network architectures, including faster packet forwarding, reduced network congestion, enhanced security, and simplified network management. By configuring layer 3 functionality, defining layer 3 interfaces, implementing routing protocols, and applying advanced features such as ACLs and QoS policies, administrators can create a robust and efficient multilayer switching environment capable of meeting the demands of today's network-intensive applications and services. Through proper configuration, monitoring, and optimization, organizations can maximize the benefits of multilayer switching and ensure the reliability and performance of their network infrastructure.

Layer 3 switching presents numerous advantages in modern networking environments due to its ability to combine the functionalities of both layer 2 switching and layer 3 routing within a single device. This integration offers significant benefits such as improved network performance, enhanced scalability, simplified network design, and reduced network congestion. Layer 3 switching operates at the network layer of the OSI model and utilizes routing information to make forwarding decisions based on IP addresses, allowing for more efficient packet processing and faster data transmission.

The setup of layer 3 switching typically involves configuring layer 3 functionality on network switches capable of supporting routing capabilities. Cisco Catalyst switches, for example, offer layer 3 switching capabilities and can be configured to perform routing functions in addition to their standard layer 2 switching capabilities. To enable layer 3 functionality on a Cisco Catalyst switch, administrators must first enter global configuration mode using the "configure terminal" command and then enable IP routing using the "ip routing" command.

arduinoCopy code

```
switch(config)# configure terminal  switch(config)# ip routing
```

In this configuration, the "ip routing" command activates layer 3 IP routing on the switch, allowing it to route traffic between different network segments based on IP addresses.

Once IP routing is enabled, administrators can configure layer 3 interfaces on the switch to facilitate routing between different network segments or VLANs. Layer 3 interfaces can be configured on switch virtual interfaces (SVIs) for VLANs or on physical interfaces for routed ports. To configure a layer 3 interface for a VLAN using an SVI, administrators can use the following CLI commands:

arduinoCopy code

switch(config)# interface vlan <vlan-id> switch(config-if)# ip address <ip-address> <subnet-mask> switch(config-if)# no shutdown

These commands configure a switch virtual interface for the specified VLAN, assign an IP address and subnet mask to the interface, and enable the interface for operation.

Alternatively, administrators can configure layer 3 interfaces on physical ports to create routed ports, allowing for direct routing between different network segments without the need for VLANs. To configure a routed port on a physical interface, administrators can use the following CLI commands:

arduinoCopy code

switch(config)# interface <interface-id> switch(config-if)# no switchport switch(config-if)# ip address <ip-address> <subnet-mask> switch(config-if)# no shutdown

In these commands, "<interface-id>" specifies the physical interface, "no switchport" removes the layer 2 switching functionality from the interface, and "<ip-address>" and "<subnet-mask>" specify the IP address and subnet mask assigned to the interface.

After configuring layer 3 interfaces, administrators can define static routes or configure dynamic routing protocols to facilitate routing between different network segments. Static routes are manually configured routes that specify the next-hop IP address or outgoing interface for destination networks. Dynamic routing protocols, such as Routing Information Protocol

(RIP), Enhanced Interior Gateway Routing Protocol (EIGRP), or Open Shortest Path First (OSPF), automatically exchange routing information between routers to dynamically update routing tables and determine the best path to reach destination networks.

To configure a static route on a Cisco Catalyst switch, administrators can use the following CLI command:

arduinoCopy code

```
switch(config)# ip route <destination-network> <subnet-mask> <next-hop-ip>
```

In this command, "<destination-network>" specifies the destination network or host, "<subnet-mask>" specifies the subnet mask for the destination network, and "<next-hop-ip>" specifies the IP address of the next-hop router or gateway.

Alternatively, administrators can configure dynamic routing protocols to enable automatic route propagation and dynamic route updates. The specific configuration commands for dynamic routing protocols may vary depending on the protocol used and the network environment.

In addition to facilitating inter-VLAN routing and inter-subnet communication, layer 3 switching offers several advantages over traditional layer 2 switching. One of the primary advantages is improved network performance and scalability. Layer 3 switches can make forwarding decisions based on IP addresses, allowing for faster packet processing and reduced network congestion compared to layer 2 switches, which make forwarding decisions based on MAC addresses. By routing traffic at the network layer, layer 3 switches can segment the network into smaller broadcast domains, reducing the scope of broadcast traffic and improving overall network efficiency.

Another advantage of layer 3 switching is simplified network design and management. By integrating routing and switching functions into a single device, layer 3 switches eliminate the need for separate routers and switches in the network topology, reducing hardware costs and simplifying network architecture. Additionally, layer 3 switches offer enhanced flexibility and scalability, allowing administrators to easily add or remove VLANs and adjust routing configurations as needed to accommodate changes in network requirements.

Furthermore, layer 3 switching provides enhanced security features compared to layer 2 switching. By enforcing access control lists (ACLs) and implementing security policies at the network layer, layer 3 switches can restrict traffic based on IP addresses, protocols, or port numbers, providing granular control over network traffic and enhancing network security. Additionally, layer 3 switches can implement virtual private networks (VPNs) and other advanced security features to protect sensitive data and ensure secure communication between remote sites.

Chapter 10: Virtual Switching System (VSS) Implementation and Management

Virtual Switching System (VSS) architecture is a Cisco innovation designed to enhance network availability, scalability, and operational efficiency by combining multiple physical switches into a single logical switch entity. This technology enables network administrators to simplify network management, improve network resiliency, and scale network capacity to meet evolving business needs.

The VSS architecture consists of two physical switches, referred to as the VSS chassis, operating in a pair. These switches work together to form a single logical switch, providing redundancy and load balancing capabilities. In a VSS configuration, one switch acts as the active supervisor, while the other serves as the standby supervisor. Both switches share a common control plane, enabling them to operate as a unified system.

To configure VSS on Cisco Catalyst switches, administrators must first ensure that the switches support VSS technology and are compatible with the desired software version. Once confirmed, the configuration process involves several steps to set up the VSS chassis, configure the VSS link, and enable VSS operation.

The first step in configuring VSS is to prepare the physical switches by installing the necessary hardware components and connecting them together using the

VSS link. The VSS link, also known as the Virtual Switch Link (VSL), is a special-purpose interconnect that facilitates communication between the two switches and synchronizes their state information.

To configure the VSS link, administrators must connect the switches using dedicated ports and configure them as VSL ports. The following CLI commands demonstrate how to configure the VSS link on Cisco Catalyst switches:

arduinoCopy code

```
switch(config)#     interface     tengigabitethernet
<module/port>     switch(config-if)#     switchport
switch(config-if)#     switchport     mode     trunk
switch(config-if)#  channel-group  <channel-number>
mode on  switch(config-if)# exit
```

In these commands, "<module/port>" specifies the physical interface on the switch, "<channel-number>" specifies the port channel number used for the VSL, and the "switchport mode trunk" command configures the interface as a trunk port to carry VLAN traffic.

Once the VSS link is configured, administrators can proceed to enable VSS on the switches. This involves configuring the switches to operate in VSS mode and synchronizing their configurations to ensure consistency across the VSS chassis.

To enable VSS mode on Cisco Catalyst switches, administrators can use the following CLI commands:

arduinoCopy code

```
switch(config)#  switch  virtual  domain  <domain-id>
switch(config-virtual)#  switch  <switch-id>  priority
```

<priority> switch(config-virtual)# switch <switch-id> role <role>

In these commands, "<domain-id>" specifies the VSS domain identifier, "<switch-id>" specifies the switch identifier (1 or 2), "<priority>" specifies the switch priority for redundancy purposes, and "<role>" specifies the role of the switch (active or standby).

After configuring VSS mode, administrators must synchronize the configurations between the two switches to ensure consistency. This involves copying the configuration from the active switch to the standby switch using the "copy running-config startup-config" command and vice versa.

luaCopy code

```
switch# copy running-config startup-config
```

With VSS configured and synchronized, the switches operate as a single logical entity, providing network redundancy and load balancing capabilities. In the event of a failure or maintenance activity, VSS allows traffic to seamlessly failover between the active and standby switches, minimizing network downtime and ensuring continuous operation.

Moreover, VSS simplifies network management by consolidating the configuration and management of the two switches into a single entity. Administrators can configure and monitor the VSS chassis using standard Cisco IOS commands, eliminating the need to manage each switch individually.

Additionally, VSS enhances network scalability by allowing administrators to add or remove switches from the VSS domain as needed without disrupting network operation. This flexibility enables organizations to easily expand their network infrastructure to accommodate growth or changes in network requirements.

In summary, VSS architecture offers significant benefits for network administrators seeking to improve network availability, scalability, and operational efficiency. By combining multiple physical switches into a single logical entity, VSS provides redundancy, load balancing, and simplified management capabilities. Through careful configuration and deployment, organizations can leverage VSS technology to build resilient and scalable network infrastructures that meet the demands of today's dynamic business environments.

VSS (Virtual Switching System) management and troubleshooting techniques are crucial aspects of maintaining the stability, performance, and reliability of network infrastructures leveraging this technology. Effective management ensures proper configuration, monitoring, and optimization of VSS deployments, while troubleshooting techniques help diagnose and resolve issues that may arise during operation.

Management of VSS configurations involves various tasks, including initial setup, ongoing maintenance, and optimization of VSS deployments. Administrators typically utilize Cisco IOS commands to perform these tasks efficiently. For instance, to verify the status of VSS on Cisco Catalyst switches, the "show switch virtual" command provides essential information such as the VSS domain ID, switch role (active or standby), and redundancy status.

arduinoCopy code

```
switch# show switch virtual
```

This command displays detailed information about the VSS configuration and the operational status of the active and standby switches. It is a fundamental tool for monitoring the health and performance of VSS deployments.

Additionally, administrators can use the "show switch virtual link" command to verify the status of the VSS link and ensure proper communication between the VSS chassis. This command provides insights into the link state, bandwidth utilization, and any errors or anomalies affecting VSS operation.

phpCopy code

```
switch# show switch virtual link
```

By regularly monitoring the VSS link status, administrators can identify potential issues and take proactive measures to prevent network downtime or performance degradation.

Another essential aspect of VSS management is software maintenance and upgrades. Cisco regularly releases new software versions to address security vulnerabilities, introduce new features, and improve overall system stability. Administrators should adhere to best practices for software maintenance, including performing regular backups of the VSS configuration, testing software updates in a lab environment before deployment, and scheduling maintenance windows to minimize disruption to network operations.

Troubleshooting VSS deployments requires a systematic approach to identify and resolve issues effectively.

When encountering network problems, administrators can use diagnostic commands to gather information about the VSS configuration, interface status, and network traffic patterns. For instance, the "show interfaces" command provides detailed statistics and status information for all interfaces on the VSS switches, allowing administrators to identify interface errors, collisions, or packet drops that may indicate underlying issues.

arduinoCopy code

switch# show interfaces

By analyzing interface statistics and error counters, administrators can pinpoint potential sources of network problems and take appropriate corrective actions, such as resetting interfaces, replacing faulty cables, or adjusting configuration parameters.

Furthermore, troubleshooting VSS deployments often involves verifying the consistency of configurations between the active and standby switches. Administrators can use the "show running-config" command to compare the running configurations of both switches and ensure they are synchronized properly. Any discrepancies or inconsistencies between the configurations may indicate configuration errors or synchronization issues that require further investigation and resolution.

arduinoCopy code

switch# show running-config

Additionally, administrators can leverage diagnostic tools such as packet captures and traffic analysis to identify and troubleshoot network issues. For instance, the "monitor session" command allows administrators to configure port mirroring or SPAN (Switched Port Analyzer) sessions to capture network traffic for analysis using external packet capture tools like Wireshark.

arduinoCopy code

```
switch# monitor session 1 source interface GigabitEthernet1/0/1 switch# monitor session 1 destination interface GigabitEthernet1/0/2
```

By capturing and analyzing network traffic, administrators can identify abnormal patterns, protocol errors, or network anomalies that may impact VSS performance and reliability.

In summary, effective management and troubleshooting techniques are essential for ensuring the stability and performance of VSS deployments. By utilizing Cisco IOS commands, diagnostic tools, and best practices, administrators can efficiently manage VSS configurations, diagnose network issues, and resolve problems to maintain the integrity and availability of their network infrastructures.

BOOK 3
ADVANCED ROUTING PROTOCOLS
MASTERING COMPLEX NETWORK CONFIGURATIONS

ROB BOTWRIGHT

Chapter 1: Overview of Routing Protocols

Routing protocols play a fundamental role in the operation of computer networks, facilitating the exchange of routing information between routers to determine optimal paths for packet forwarding. There are several types of routing protocols, each designed to address specific network requirements and characteristics. These protocols can be categorized based on various criteria, including their routing algorithm, behavior, and deployment environment. Understanding the different types of routing protocols is essential for network administrators and engineers tasked with designing, implementing, and managing network infrastructures.

One common way to classify routing protocols is based on their routing algorithm, which determines how routers calculate and maintain routing tables. Distance vector routing protocols, such as RIP (Routing Information Protocol) and RIPv2, use a simple algorithm to exchange routing information with neighboring routers and calculate the shortest path to destination networks based on hop count. These protocols periodically broadcast routing updates to neighboring routers, making them suitable for small to medium-sized networks with relatively simple topologies. Administrators can configure distance vector routing protocols using commands such as "router rip" in Cisco

IOS to enable RIP routing on routers and specify routing parameters.

Copy code

```
router rip
```

Another type of routing protocol is link-state routing protocols, which include OSPF (Open Shortest Path First) and IS-IS (Intermediate System to Intermediate System). Unlike distance vector protocols, link-state protocols use a more sophisticated algorithm to build a detailed network topology map and calculate the shortest path to destination networks based on various metrics such as bandwidth, delay, and reliability. These protocols exchange link-state advertisements (LSAs) to communicate routing information and maintain synchronized routing databases among routers. Administrators can configure OSPF routing using commands such as "router ospf" in Cisco IOS to enable OSPF routing on routers and specify OSPF areas, authentication, and other parameters.

arduinoCopy code

```
router ospf <process-id>
```

A third category of routing protocols is path-vector routing protocols, which include BGP (Border Gateway Protocol). Path-vector protocols are commonly used in large-scale networks, such as the Internet, where routers need to make routing decisions based on policy considerations, network policies, and external factors. BGP is a complex and highly flexible protocol that allows administrators to implement sophisticated routing policies and control the flow of traffic between autonomous systems (ASes). Configuring BGP routing involves commands such as "router bgp" in Cisco IOS to enable BGP routing on routers and specify BGP neighbors, autonomous system numbers (ASNs), and route filtering policies.

phpCopy code

```
router bgp <asn>
```

Routing protocols can also be classified based on their behavior and deployment environment. Interior gateway protocols (IGPs) are routing protocols designed for use within a single autonomous system (AS) and are responsible for exchanging routing information between routers within the same administrative domain. Examples of IGPs include RIP, OSPF, and EIGRP (Enhanced Interior Gateway Routing Protocol). Exterior gateway protocols (EGPs), on the other hand, are routing protocols used to exchange routing information between different autonomous systems (ASes) and are typically used at the edge of the Internet to connect different Internet service providers (ISPs) and large organizations. BGP is the primary EGP used on the Internet.

In addition to their algorithm and behavior, routing protocols can also be classified based on their support for various network technologies and features. For example, some routing protocols are designed to support IPv4 networks, while others are IPv6-capable. Similarly, some protocols support features such as authentication, route summarization, and load balancing, while others may lack these capabilities.

Overall, the choice of routing protocol depends on various factors, including the size and complexity of the network, the network's traffic patterns and requirements, the availability of network resources, and the organization's network design goals and policies. By understanding the different types of routing protocols and their characteristics, network administrators and engineers can select the most appropriate routing protocol(s) for their specific network environment and requirements, ensuring efficient and reliable packet routing and delivery.

Routing protocol selection is a critical decision in network design, as it directly impacts the performance, scalability, and resilience of the network infrastructure. When choosing a routing protocol, network administrators and engineers must consider various factors and criteria to ensure that the selected protocol meets the specific requirements and goals of the network. These criteria encompass technical considerations, such as routing protocol features, scalability, convergence time, and resource utilization, as well as operational factors like network complexity, administrative overhead, and support for network policies.

One of the primary criteria for routing protocol selection is the scalability of the protocol, which refers to its ability to handle large and complex networks with thousands of routers and subnets efficiently. Scalability is crucial for networks that are expected to grow over time or that span multiple geographic locations. Routing protocols like OSPF (Open Shortest Path First) and IS-IS (Intermediate System to Intermediate System) are often preferred for large-scale networks due to their hierarchical design, support for multiple areas, and efficient flooding mechanisms. These protocols allow administrators to partition the network into smaller domains, reducing the size of routing tables and minimizing the impact of topology changes on network convergence.

Another important consideration is the convergence time of the routing protocol, which refers to the speed at which routers can adapt to changes in network topology and update their routing tables accordingly. Fast convergence is essential for minimizing network downtime and ensuring uninterrupted service delivery, particularly in mission-critical environments. Routing protocols like EIGRP (Enhanced Interior Gateway Routing Protocol) and IS-IS are known for their fast convergence capabilities, thanks to features such as incremental updates, triggered updates, and optimized data structures. These protocols can quickly propagate routing information and recalculate paths in response to link failures or network topology changes, reducing the time it takes for routers to converge on new routes.

Additionally, administrators must consider the resource utilization of the routing protocol, including factors such as CPU and memory overhead, bandwidth consumption, and network traffic overhead. Some routing protocols generate more control traffic than others, which can lead to increased network congestion and resource consumption, particularly in large-scale deployments. For example, distance vector protocols like RIP (Routing Information Protocol) periodically broadcast routing updates to all neighbors, resulting in higher control traffic overhead compared to link-state protocols like OSPF, which only send updates when topology changes occur. By evaluating the resource utilization of different routing protocols, administrators can ensure that the chosen protocol is suitable for the network's capacity and resource constraints.

Another critical factor in routing protocol selection is the support for network policies and requirements. Different routing protocols offer varying degrees of flexibility and support for features such as route summarization, route filtering, policy-based routing, and authentication. For example, BGP (Border Gateway Protocol) is commonly used in large-scale networks and the Internet due to its advanced policy capabilities, which allow administrators to implement complex routing policies and control the flow of traffic between autonomous systems (ASes). In contrast, IGPs (Interior Gateway Protocols) like OSPF and EIGRP are more suitable for internal networks, offering features such as route summarization and route redistribution to support hierarchical routing and policy enforcement.

Administrative overhead and complexity are also important considerations in routing protocol selection. Some protocols require more configuration and maintenance than others, which can increase operational complexity and the risk of misconfiguration. For example, OSPF is known for its complexity and requires careful planning and design to ensure proper operation, particularly in large networks with multiple areas and complex topologies. In contrast, protocols like

RIP are simpler to configure but may lack advanced features and scalability, making them less suitable for larger or more complex networks. Administrators must weigh the trade-offs between protocol complexity and features to choose the most appropriate protocol for their network environment.

Moreover, compatibility and interoperability with existing network infrastructure and devices are essential considerations in routing protocol selection. Administrators must ensure that the chosen protocol is supported by their network equipment, including routers, switches, and other networking devices. Additionally, interoperability with other routing protocols and network technologies, such as MPLS (Multiprotocol Label Switching) and VPN (Virtual Private Network) technologies, may be necessary to support specific network requirements or integration with third-party systems and services.

In summary, routing protocol selection is a multifaceted process that requires careful consideration of various technical and operational factors. By evaluating criteria such as scalability, convergence time, resource utilization, support for network policies, administrative overhead, and compatibility, administrators can choose the most suitable routing protocol(s) to meet the needs and objectives of their network environment. This ensures efficient routing, optimal network performance, and reliable service delivery, enabling organizations to build robust and resilient network infrastructures that support their business goals and objectives.

Chapter 2: Advanced OSPF (Open Shortest Path First) Configuration

OSPF (Open Shortest Path First) is a popular link-state routing protocol used in large-scale networks to efficiently exchange routing information and calculate optimal paths between routers. One of the key features of OSPF is its support for hierarchical design through the use of areas. OSPF divides a network into multiple areas, each serving a specific purpose and containing a subset of routers and links. This hierarchical design offers several benefits, including scalability, reduced routing overhead, improved convergence, and enhanced security.

To deploy OSPF areas, network administrators first divide the network into logical segments based on factors such as geographic location, network size, and administrative boundaries. Each area is assigned a unique identifier known as an Area ID, which is a 32-bit number used to distinguish between areas within the OSPF domain. The backbone area, also known as Area 0, is a special area that serves as the core of the OSPF domain and connects all other areas within the network. It provides transit services for routing information between non-backbone areas and ensures connectivity and reachability throughout the OSPF domain.

Administrators configure OSPF areas on routers using the "area" command in OSPF configuration mode. For example, to configure a router to belong to Area 1, the administrator would enter the following command:

Copy code

```
router ospf 1 area 1
```

Once OSPF areas are configured, routers within the same area exchange link-state advertisements (LSAs) to build a detailed topology map of the area. This information is used to calculate the shortest path to destination networks and update the routers' routing tables accordingly. Routers in different areas exchange summarized routing information, known as inter-area routes, through the backbone area. This hierarchical routing structure reduces the size of routing tables and minimizes routing overhead, particularly in large networks with hundreds or thousands of routers.

In addition to scalability and reduced overhead, OSPF areas also improve network convergence by isolating changes in network topology to specific areas. When a link or router failure occurs within an area, OSPF routers within that area recalculate routes and update their routing tables without affecting routers in other areas. This localized computation reduces the impact of network disruptions and speeds up convergence, ensuring that routing updates are propagated quickly and accurately throughout the OSPF domain.

Furthermore, OSPF areas enhance network security by controlling the propagation of routing information and isolating network traffic within specific areas. Administrators can implement access control policies and route filtering within areas to restrict the exchange of routing updates and prevent unauthorized access to sensitive network resources. By segmenting the network into areas, organizations can limit the scope of potential network attacks and minimize the risk of unauthorized access or data breaches.

Another advantage of OSPF areas is their support for network growth and evolution. As the network expands or undergoes changes, administrators can add new areas or adjust existing area boundaries to accommodate growth and optimize network performance. OSPF allows for flexible area design, enabling administrators to tailor the network topology to meet changing business requirements and adapt to evolving technology trends.

In summary, OSPF areas and hierarchical design are essential components of large-scale network architectures, providing scalability, efficiency, resilience, and security. By dividing the network into logical segments and organizing routers into areas, OSPF minimizes routing overhead, improves convergence, enhances security, and supports network growth. Network administrators can leverage OSPF areas to build robust and resilient network infrastructures that meet the needs of modern enterprises and ensure reliable service delivery in dynamic and evolving environments.

OSPF (Open Shortest Path First) is a powerful routing protocol that offers a wide range of advanced configuration options to fine-tune its behavior and optimize network performance. These advanced options allow network administrators to customize

OSPF operation according to specific requirements, improve routing efficiency, enhance network stability, and address unique deployment scenarios. Understanding and effectively utilizing these advanced configuration options is essential for maximizing the benefits of OSPF in complex network environments.

One of the key advanced configuration options in OSPF is the ability to adjust the OSPF cost metric for individual interfaces. The OSPF cost metric determines the relative preference for routes and influences the path selection process. By adjusting the cost metric, administrators can influence the selection of preferred paths through the network. This can be particularly useful in scenarios where specific paths need to be favored over others, such as for optimizing traffic flow or load balancing.

To configure the OSPF cost metric for an interface, administrators can use the "ip ospf cost" command in interface configuration mode. For example, to set the OSPF cost metric for GigabitEthernet0/1 to 10, the following command can be used:

kotlinCopy code

interface GigabitEthernet0/1 ip ospf cost 10

Another important aspect of OSPF advanced configuration is the fine-tuning of OSPF timers. OSPF relies on various timers to control the frequency of routing updates, the duration of neighbor adjacencies, and the convergence time in response to network changes. Adjusting these timers can have a significant impact on OSPF operation, affecting factors such as routing stability, convergence speed, and resource utilization.

The key OSPF timers that can be adjusted include the hello interval, dead interval, and LSA (Link-State Advertisement) retransmission interval. The hello interval controls how often OSPF routers send hello packets to discover and maintain neighbor adjacencies, while the dead interval specifies the duration of time before a router considers a neighbor to be unreachable. By adjusting these timers, administrators can fine-tune OSPF convergence behavior and responsiveness to network events.

To configure OSPF timers, administrators can use the relevant commands in OSPF configuration mode. For example, to set the hello interval to 5 seconds and the dead interval to 20 seconds for OSPF process 1, the following commands can be used:

Copy code

```
router ospf 1 timers hello 5 timers dead 20
```

In addition to adjusting timers, OSPF supports various authentication mechanisms to secure routing information exchange between OSPF routers. Authentication ensures that only trusted routers can participate in OSPF routing and prevents unauthorized devices from injecting false routing information into the network. OSPF supports several authentication methods, including plain text authentication, MD5 authentication, and IPsec authentication.

To configure OSPF authentication, administrators can use the "ip ospf authentication" command in OSPF interface configuration mode. For example, to configure

MD5 authentication with a pre-shared key on GigabitEthernet0/1 for OSPF process 1, the following commands can be used:

kotlinCopy code

interface GigabitEthernet0/1 ip ospf authentication message-digest ip ospf message-digest-key 1 md5 SECRETKEY

Moreover, OSPF provides advanced options for route summarization and filtering to control the propagation of routing information and reduce the size of routing tables. Route summarization allows administrators to aggregate multiple routes into a single summary route, which can help minimize routing overhead and improve network scalability. Additionally, OSPF supports route filtering to selectively advertise or suppress specific routes based on predefined criteria, such as prefix lists, access control lists (ACLs), or route maps.

To configure route summarization in OSPF, administrators can use the "summary-address" command in OSPF router configuration mode. For example, to summarize routes for networks 192.168.1.0/24 and 192.168.2.0/24 into a single summary route for advertisement in OSPF process 1, the following command can be used:

cssCopy code

router ospf 1 summary-address 192.168.0.0 255.255.252.0

Similarly, OSPF route filtering can be configured using access control lists (ACLs) or route maps to permit or deny the advertisement of specific routes. For example,

to filter out routes for network 10.0.0.0/24 from being advertised in OSPF process 1, the following access control list and distribute-list command can be used:
csharpCopy code

```
access-list 1 deny 10.0.0.0 0.0.0.255 router ospf 1
distribute-list 1 out
```

In summary, OSPF offers a wide range of advanced configuration options to customize routing behavior, optimize network performance, and enhance security. By leveraging these advanced features, administrators can fine-tune OSPF operation according to specific requirements and ensure efficient and reliable routing in complex network environments. Understanding how to deploy and configure OSPF advanced options is essential for building scalable, resilient, and secure networks that meet the demands of modern enterprise environments.

Chapter 3: EIGRP (Enhanced Interior Gateway Routing Protocol) Optimization

EIGRP (Enhanced Interior Gateway Routing Protocol) is a sophisticated routing protocol developed by Cisco Systems to provide efficient and scalable routing in enterprise networks. Unlike traditional distance vector protocols, such as RIP (Routing Information Protocol), EIGRP uses a hybrid routing algorithm that combines aspects of both distance vector and link-state protocols. This unique approach offers several advanced features and benefits that make EIGRP a popular choice for network administrators seeking fast convergence, low overhead, and support for large-scale networks.

One of the key features of EIGRP is its support for both IPv4 and IPv6 routing, allowing organizations to transition to IPv6 seamlessly without requiring significant changes to their routing infrastructure. EIGRP for IPv4 and EIGRP for IPv6 share many similarities in terms of operation and configuration, making it easy for administrators to manage routing for mixed IPv4/IPv6 networks.

To deploy EIGRP in a network, administrators first enable the EIGRP routing process on routers using the "router eigrp" command in global configuration mode. They specify the autonomous system number (ASN) as a parameter, which identifies the EIGRP routing domain. For example, to enable EIGRP process 100 on a router, the following command can be used:

Copy code

```
router eigrp 100
```

Once the EIGRP process is enabled, administrators configure EIGRP neighbors by specifying the adjacent routers' IP addresses using the "neighbor" command in EIGRP router configuration mode. This informs the router of its neighboring EIGRP routers and initiates the formation of EIGRP neighbor adjacencies. For example, to configure a neighbor relationship with a router with IP address 192.168.1.1, the following command can be used:

Copy code

```
router eigrp 100 neighbor 192.168.1.1
```

EIGRP uses a sophisticated metric called the composite metric, which considers multiple factors such as bandwidth, delay, reliability, and load when calculating the best path to a destination network. By default, EIGRP uses bandwidth and delay as its composite metric components, but administrators can customize the metric calculation by adjusting the weights assigned to each component. This allows administrators to prioritize certain network characteristics over others when selecting the best path.

To configure EIGRP metric weights, administrators use the "metric weights" command in EIGRP router configuration mode. They specify the weights for bandwidth, delay, reliability, and load as parameters, controlling how each component contributes to the overall metric calculation. For example, to prioritize bandwidth over delay in EIGRP metric calculation, the following command can be used:

Copy code

```
router eigrp 100 metric weights 0 1 0 0 0 0
```

EIGRP also supports route summarization, which allows administrators to aggregate multiple routes into a single summary route, reducing the size of routing tables and minimizing routing overhead. Route summarization is particularly useful in large-scale networks with complex topologies, as it simplifies routing table management and improves network scalability.

To configure route summarization in EIGRP, administrators use the "summary-address" command in EIGRP router configuration mode. They specify the summary route prefix and subnet mask as parameters, defining the range of routes to be summarized. For example, to summarize routes for networks 192.168.1.0/24 and 192.168.2.0/24 into a single summary route for advertisement, the following command can be used:

cssCopy code

```
router eigrp 100 summary-address 192.168.0.0 255.255.252.0
```

Another advanced feature of EIGRP is its support for unequal-cost load balancing, which allows traffic to be distributed across multiple unequal-cost paths to the same destination network. This enhances network efficiency and improves resource utilization by utilizing available bandwidth more effectively.

To enable unequal-cost load balancing in EIGRP, administrators use the "variance" command in EIGRP router configuration mode. They specify a multiplier value as a parameter, which determines the maximum tolerated difference in path costs for load balancing. For example, to enable unequal-cost load balancing with a variance of 2, the following command can be used:

Copy code

```
router eigrp 100 variance 2
```

Furthermore, EIGRP provides mechanisms for route filtering and policy-based routing, allowing administrators to control the advertisement and propagation of routing information based on specific criteria. Route filtering can be implemented using access control lists (ACLs) or prefix lists to permit or deny the advertisement of routes matching certain characteristics. Policy-based routing allows administrators to define policies that dictate the forwarding behavior for packets based on predefined criteria, such as source or destination IP addresses.

In summary, EIGRP offers a rich set of advanced features and capabilities that make it a versatile and powerful routing protocol for enterprise networks. From support for IPv6 routing to advanced metric customization, route summarization, unequal-cost load balancing, and route filtering, EIGRP provides administrators with the tools they need to optimize routing performance, scalability, and efficiency in diverse network environments. Understanding how to leverage these features effectively is essential for deploying and managing EIGRP-based networks successfully.

Tuning EIGRP metrics for performance is a crucial aspect of optimizing routing in enterprise networks. EIGRP

(Enhanced Interior Gateway Routing Protocol) provides various metrics that determine the best path to destination networks. By adjusting these metrics, network administrators can influence routing decisions, enhance network performance, and achieve better utilization of network resources.

The metric used by EIGRP to calculate the best path to a destination network is the composite metric. This metric takes into account several factors, including bandwidth, delay, reliability, and load. Each of these factors contributes to the overall metric calculation, and by adjusting their values, administrators can prioritize certain characteristics over others when selecting the best path.

To adjust EIGRP metrics for performance tuning, administrators typically focus on bandwidth and delay, as these are the primary components of the composite metric. Bandwidth represents the available capacity of a network link, while delay measures the time it takes for data packets to traverse the link. By modifying these values, administrators can influence routing decisions and optimize network performance.

In EIGRP, the bandwidth and delay metrics are configured on individual interfaces. The bandwidth metric is expressed in kilobits per second (kbps), while the delay metric is specified in tens of microseconds (tens of µs). Administrators can adjust these metrics based on the characteristics of the network links and their desired routing behavior.

To configure the bandwidth metric on an interface in EIGRP, administrators use the "bandwidth" command in interface configuration mode. For example, to set the bandwidth of GigabitEthernet0/1 to 100 Mbps, the following command can be used:

kotlinCopy code

interface GigabitEthernet0/1 bandwidth 100000

Similarly, to configure the delay metric on an interface, administrators use the "delay" command in interface configuration mode. The delay value is specified in tens of microseconds. For example, to set the delay of GigabitEthernet0/1 to 10 microseconds, the following command can be used:

kotlinCopy code

interface GigabitEthernet0/1 delay 1000

By adjusting the bandwidth and delay metrics on network interfaces, administrators can influence the calculation of the composite metric and control the selection of the best path for routing. For example, increasing the bandwidth metric on a high-speed link can make it more attractive for routing, while adjusting the delay metric can influence the selection of paths based on latency considerations.

In addition to adjusting bandwidth and delay metrics, administrators can also fine-tune other aspects of EIGRP operation to further optimize network performance. For example, adjusting the EIGRP timers can affect the frequency of routing updates and the convergence time in response to network changes. By optimizing these timers, administrators can reduce routing overhead and improve the responsiveness of the network.

To configure EIGRP timers, administrators use the "timers" command in EIGRP router configuration mode.

They can adjust the hello interval, dead interval, and other timers to suit the requirements of their network environment. For example, to set the hello interval to 5 seconds and the dead interval to 20 seconds for EIGRP process 1, the following commands can be used:

Copy code

```
router eigrp 1 timers hello 5 timers dead 20
```

Furthermore, administrators can leverage route summarization and filtering techniques to optimize EIGRP routing tables and reduce routing overhead. Route summarization involves aggregating multiple routes into a single summary route, while route filtering allows administrators to selectively advertise or suppress specific routes based on predefined criteria.

To configure route summarization in EIGRP, administrators use the "summary-address" command in EIGRP router configuration mode. They specify the summary route prefix and subnet mask to define the range of routes to be summarized. For example, to summarize routes for networks 192.168.1.0/24 and 192.168.2.0/24 into a single summary route for advertisement, the following command can be used:

cssCopy code

```
router eigrp 1 summary-address 192.168.0.0
255.255.252.0
```

Similarly, route filtering can be configured using access control lists (ACLs) or prefix lists to permit or deny the advertisement of specific routes. By implementing route summarization and filtering, administrators can optimize the size of EIGRP routing tables and improve routing efficiency.

In summary, tuning EIGRP metrics for performance is essential for optimizing routing in enterprise networks. By adjusting bandwidth and delay metrics, optimizing EIGRP timers, and leveraging route summarization and filtering techniques, administrators can enhance network performance, improve resource utilization, and achieve efficient routing operation. Understanding how to deploy these techniques effectively is critical for maximizing the benefits of EIGRP in complex network environments.

Chapter 4: BGP (Border Gateway Protocol) Essentials

BGP (Border Gateway Protocol) is a fundamental protocol used in the Internet to exchange routing information between different autonomous systems (ASes). Unlike interior gateway protocols such as OSPF or EIGRP, BGP is an exterior gateway protocol designed to facilitate interdomain routing and maintain connectivity between disparate networks. BGP operates on TCP (Transmission Control Protocol) port 179 and employs a path-vector routing algorithm to make routing decisions based on network policies and attributes rather than just shortest path. This makes BGP well-suited for large-scale networks with complex routing policies and diverse connectivity requirements.

To deploy BGP in a network, administrators first need to configure BGP neighbors or peers. This is achieved by using the "neighbor" command in BGP router configuration mode, specifying the IP address of the neighboring router. For example, to establish a BGP neighbor relationship with a router with IP address 192.168.1.1, the following command can be used:

phpCopy code

router bgp <AS_number> neighbor 192.168.1.1 remote-as <neighbor_AS_number>

In BGP, each router participating in the protocol must belong to an autonomous system (AS) and have a unique AS number. When configuring BGP neighbors, administrators must specify the AS number of the neighboring router using the "remote-as" parameter.

Once BGP neighbor relationships are established, routers exchange routing information in the form of BGP update messages. These messages contain network reachability information along with various attributes such as AS path, next hop, and prefix length. BGP routers use this information to build a routing table and make forwarding decisions.

One of the key functions of BGP is route selection based on policy. Unlike interior gateway protocols that primarily use metrics like cost or hop count to select the best path, BGP allows administrators to define routing policies based on various attributes such as AS path, origin, and community. These policies determine how BGP routes are selected and propagated throughout the network.

In BGP, route selection is based on the BGP decision process, which evaluates multiple attributes in a predetermined order. The first attribute considered is the "weight," which is a Cisco-specific parameter used to influence route preference locally on a router. Higher-weighted routes are preferred over lower-weighted routes.

If routes have the same weight, the next attribute considered is the "local preference." Local preference is an attribute assigned to incoming routes to indicate their preference within an AS. Higher local preference values indicate more preferred routes, and routes with higher local preference values are selected for forwarding.

If routes have the same local preference, the next attribute considered is the "AS path." The AS path attribute represents the sequence of AS numbers that a route has traversed to reach the router. BGP prefers routes with shorter AS paths, as they indicate fewer AS hops to reach the destination.

In addition to the AS path, BGP also considers other attributes such as the origin, which indicates how the route was learned (i.e., whether it was originated within the local AS or learned from an external source), and the MED (Multi-Exit Discriminator), which is used to influence routing decisions between multiple exit points from an AS.

Administrators can manipulate these attributes using various techniques such as route maps, prefix lists, and AS path access lists to implement routing policies and control the flow of traffic within the network. For example, administrators can use route maps to set the local preference for specific routes or prepend AS numbers to influence the AS path attribute.

Furthermore, BGP supports route aggregation, which allows multiple contiguous IP prefixes to be summarized into a single aggregate route. Route aggregation helps reduce the size of BGP routing tables and minimize the amount of routing information exchanged between BGP peers.

To configure route aggregation in BGP, administrators use the "aggregate-address" command in BGP router configuration mode. They specify the summary prefix and subnet mask as parameters, defining the range of routes to be aggregated. For example, to aggregate routes for networks 192.168.1.0/24 and 192.168.2.0/24 into a single summary route, the following command can be used:

cssCopy code

router bgp <AS_number> aggregate-address 192.168.0.0 255.255.252.0

In summary, BGP is a critical protocol for interdomain routing on the Internet and plays a vital role in maintaining connectivity between autonomous systems. By understanding the basics of BGP and its functions, administrators can deploy BGP in their networks to achieve scalable, policy-driven routing and effective traffic engineering. Through the use of BGP attributes, route manipulation techniques, and route aggregation, administrators can implement sophisticated routing policies and optimize network performance.

BGP peering and routing policies are crucial components of configuring and managing a Border Gateway Protocol (BGP) network. BGP peering refers to the establishment of neighbor relationships between BGP routers to exchange routing information. These neighbor relationships can be established either within the same autonomous system (iBGP) or between different autonomous systems (eBGP). To configure BGP peering, administrators use the "neighbor" command in BGP router configuration mode, specifying the IP address of the neighboring router and its autonomous system number (ASN). For example, to establish an eBGP peering session with a neighboring router with IP address 203.0.113.1 and ASN 65001, the following command can be used:

csharpCopy code

```
router bgp <local_ASN> neighbor 203.0.113.1 remote-as 65001
```

Once BGP peering sessions are established, routers exchange routing information in the form of BGP update messages. These messages contain network reachability information along with various attributes such as the AS path, next hop, and prefix length. Routing policies in BGP are used to control the advertisement and acceptance of routes based on predefined criteria such as route preference, AS path, and community values.

One common routing policy in BGP is route filtering, which allows administrators to selectively advertise or suppress specific routes. Route filtering can be implemented using prefix lists, AS path access lists (ASPATH ACLs), or route maps. Prefix lists are used to filter routes based on their destination prefixes, while AS path access lists filter routes based on their AS path attributes. Route maps provide more granular control over route filtering and allow administrators to apply multiple filtering criteria.

To configure route filtering using prefix lists, administrators first create a prefix list specifying the prefixes to be filtered and their corresponding subnet masks. Then, they apply the prefix list to the BGP neighbor using the "neighbor distribute-list" command in BGP router configuration mode. For example, to filter routes for network 192.0.2.0/24 from being advertised to a neighboring router with IP address 203.0.113.1, the following commands can be used:

scssCopy code

ip prefix-list FILTER-192 permit 192.0.2.0/24 router bgp <local_ASN> neighbor 203.0.113.1 distribute-list prefix FILTER-192 out

Similarly, administrators can configure route filtering using AS path access lists to filter routes based on their AS path attributes. AS path access lists are configured using the "ip as-path access-list" command in global configuration mode. Once the AS path access list is created, it can be applied to the BGP neighbor using the "neighbor filter-list" command in BGP router configuration mode.

In addition to route filtering, BGP routing policies can also be used to manipulate route attributes such as the local preference, MED (Multi-Exit Discriminator), and next hop. These attributes influence route selection and path preference within the BGP network. For example, administrators can use route maps to set the local preference for specific routes or modify the MED value to influence routing decisions between multiple exit points from an autonomous system.

To configure route attribute manipulation using route maps, administrators define a route map specifying the desired actions and conditions for route modification. Then, they apply the route map to the BGP neighbor using the "neighbor route-map" command in BGP router configuration mode. For example, to set the local preference for routes received from a neighboring router with IP address 203.0.113.1 to 200, the following commands can be used:

sqlCopy code

route-map SET-PREFERENCE permit 10 match ip address prefix-list PREFIX-LIST set local-preference 200 ip prefix-list PREFIX-LIST permit 203.0.113.0/24 router bgp <local_ASN> neighbor 203.0.113.1 route-map SET-PREFERENCE in

Furthermore, BGP routing policies can also involve the use of BGP communities, which are used to group routes and apply common policies to them. BGP communities are attached to routes as they are advertised between BGP routers, allowing administrators to implement specific actions based on community values. For example, BGP communities can be used to influence route preference, control route propagation, or implement traffic engineering policies.

To configure BGP communities, administrators define community lists specifying the desired community values and their corresponding actions. Then, they apply the community list to route maps or BGP neighbors using the "neighbor route-map" or "neighbor send-community" commands in BGP router configuration mode. For example, to tag routes with a specific community value and propagate the community to a neighboring router with IP address 203.0.113.1, the following commands can be used:

sqlCopy code

ip community-list 10 permit 65001:100 route-map SET-COMMUNITY permit 10 match ip address community-list 10 set community 65001:200 router bgp <local_ASN> neighbor 203.0.113.1 send-community neighbor 203.0.113.1 route-map SET-COMMUNITY out

In summary, BGP peering and routing policies are essential for configuring and managing BGP networks. By establishing BGP peering sessions and implementing routing policies such as route filtering, attribute manipulation, and community tagging, administrators can control the flow of routing information and shape the behavior of BGP routers in the network. These techniques allow for greater flexibility, scalability, and control over BGP routing decisions, enabling administrators to optimize network performance and meet specific business requirements.

Chapter 5: Route Redistribution Strategies

Route redistribution is a fundamental concept in networking that involves the exchange of routing information between different routing protocols. In complex network environments where multiple routing protocols are used, route redistribution becomes essential for ensuring end-to-end connectivity and optimal routing. The process of route redistribution allows routers running different routing protocols to share routing information and dynamically update their routing tables, enabling seamless communication across the network.

At its core, route redistribution involves the exchange of routing information between routing domains using different routing protocols. This exchange occurs at the boundary between routing domains, typically at the point where routers running different routing protocols are connected. The objective of route redistribution is to enable routers in one routing domain to learn routes from another routing domain and vice versa, thereby facilitating end-to-end packet delivery.

To implement route redistribution, routers need to be configured to advertise routes learned from one routing protocol into another routing protocol. This is achieved through the use of redistribution commands in the router's configuration. For example, to redistribute routes learned from OSPF into the EIGRP routing process, the "redistribute ospf" command is used in EIGRP router configuration mode:

phpCopy code

router eigrp <AS_number> redistribute ospf <process_ID> metric <metric_values>

In this command, "<process_ID>" specifies the OSPF process from which routes are to be redistributed, and "<metric_values>" define the metrics assigned to redistributed routes. Similarly, routes learned from EIGRP can be redistributed into OSPF using the "redistribute eigrp" command in OSPF router configuration mode.

Route redistribution can be a complex process, particularly in heterogeneous network environments with multiple routing protocols and diverse network topologies. One of the key challenges in route redistribution is ensuring seamless route propagation without causing routing loops or suboptimal routing decisions. To address this challenge, administrators need to carefully plan and configure route redistribution policies to maintain network stability and efficiency.

One common consideration in route redistribution is the handling of route metrics and administrative distances. Different routing protocols use different metrics and administrative distances to calculate the best path to a destination. When redistributing routes between routing protocols, administrators need to ensure that route metrics are appropriately adjusted to reflect the characteristics of the receiving routing protocol. This adjustment helps prevent routing loops and ensures that redistributed routes are accurately evaluated by routers in the receiving routing domain.

In addition to metric manipulation, route redistribution policies may also involve the application of route filters to control the scope of redistributed routes. Route filters allow administrators to selectively advertise or suppress specific routes based on predefined criteria such as route prefixes, route tags, or route attributes. By applying route filters, administrators can tailor the set of redistributed routes to meet specific network requirements and constraints.

Another important consideration in route redistribution is the handling of route summarization and aggregation. Route summarization involves consolidating multiple contiguous routes into a single summarized route, which helps reduce the size of routing tables and minimize the overhead associated with route advertisement. When redistributing routes between routing protocols, administrators may choose to summarize routes to improve network scalability and efficiency.

To summarize routes during route redistribution, administrators can use the "summary-address" command in router configuration mode. This command allows administrators to define summary addresses and associated subnet masks for route aggregation. For example, to summarize routes for networks 192.168.0.0/24 and 192.168.1.0/24 into a single summary route, the following command can be used:
cssCopy code

```
router     ospf     <process_ID>     summary-address
192.168.0.0 255.255.254.0
```

By summarizing routes, administrators can reduce the size of routing updates and optimize routing table memory utilization, thereby improving network performance and scalability.

Despite its benefits, route redistribution introduces complexities and potential pitfalls that must be carefully managed. One common challenge in route redistribution is the occurrence of routing loops caused by suboptimal route selection or inconsistent route advertisements. To mitigate the risk of routing loops, administrators can implement route filtering and route tagging mechanisms to control the flow of redistributed routes and enforce routing policies.

Moreover, route redistribution can impact network convergence and stability, particularly in environments with dynamic routing protocols and frequent topology changes. Administrators need to monitor and troubleshoot route redistribution issues proactively to identify and resolve routing anomalies before they affect network operation. This may involve analyzing routing tables, examining route advertisements, and verifying route redistribution configurations using diagnostic tools such as ping, traceroute, and show commands.

In summary, route redistribution is a critical aspect of network design and operation, enabling routers running different routing protocols to exchange routing information and maintain end-to-end connectivity. By carefully planning and configuring route redistribution policies, administrators can ensure seamless communication across heterogeneous network environments while optimizing routing efficiency and scalability. However, route redistribution requires careful consideration of factors such as route metrics, route filtering, summarization, and convergence behavior to avoid routing issues and maintain network stability.

Route redistribution between protocols is a crucial aspect of network management, allowing routers to exchange routing information across diverse routing domains and protocols to ensure end-to-end connectivity and optimal routing. This process enables routers running different routing protocols to share routing information and dynamically update their routing tables, facilitating seamless communication across the network.

The process of implementing route redistribution involves configuring routers to advertise routes learned from one routing protocol into another routing protocol. This exchange occurs at the boundary between routing domains, typically where routers running different routing protocols are interconnected. By redistributing routes between protocols, routers can effectively learn and propagate routes from one domain to another, enhancing network flexibility and interoperability.

To implement route redistribution, administrators need to configure redistribution commands on routers to advertise routes learned from one routing protocol into another. For example, to redistribute routes learned from OSPF into the EIGRP routing process, administrators can use the "redistribute ospf" command in EIGRP router configuration mode:

phpCopy code

```
router eigrp <AS_number> redistribute ospf <process_ID> metric <metric_values>
```

In this command, "<process_ID>" specifies the OSPF process from which routes are to be redistributed, and "<metric_values>" define the metrics assigned to redistributed routes. Similarly, routes learned from EIGRP can be redistributed into OSPF using the "redistribute eigrp" command in OSPF router configuration mode.

One of the key considerations when implementing route redistribution is ensuring that routing information is exchanged efficiently and accurately between routing protocols. This involves configuring appropriate metrics and administrative distances to influence route selection and prevent routing loops. Administrators must carefully plan and configure redistribution policies to maintain network stability and optimize routing decisions.

Route redistribution can be complex, particularly in heterogeneous network environments with multiple routing protocols and diverse network topologies. Administrators must consider factors such as route summarization, metric manipulation, and route filtering to ensure seamless route propagation without causing routing anomalies or suboptimal routing decisions.

Route summarization is a technique used to consolidate multiple contiguous routes into a single summarized route, reducing the size of routing tables and minimizing the overhead associated with route advertisement. To summarize routes during route redistribution, administrators can use the "summary-address" command in router configuration mode to define summary addresses and associated subnet masks for route aggregation.

Route filtering allows administrators to selectively advertise or suppress specific routes based on predefined criteria such as route prefixes, route tags, or route attributes. By applying route filters, administrators can control the scope of redistributed routes and tailor the set of advertised routes to meet specific network requirements and constraints.

Another important consideration in route redistribution is the handling of route convergence and stability. Route redistribution can impact network convergence and stability, particularly in environments with dynamic routing protocols and frequent topology changes. Administrators must monitor and troubleshoot route redistribution issues proactively to identify and resolve routing anomalies before they affect network operation.

To mitigate the risk of routing loops and routing anomalies, administrators can implement route filtering and route tagging mechanisms to control the flow of redistributed routes and enforce routing policies. By carefully planning and configuring route redistribution policies, administrators can ensure seamless communication across heterogeneous network environments while optimizing routing efficiency and scalability.

In summary, route redistribution between protocols is a critical aspect of network design and operation, enabling routers to exchange routing information across diverse routing domains and protocols. By implementing effective route redistribution policies, administrators can enhance network flexibility, interoperability, and stability while optimizing routing decisions and ensuring seamless end-to-end connectivity.

Chapter 6: Advanced Route Filtering Techniques

Route filtering mechanisms play a crucial role in network management, allowing administrators to control the flow of routing information and shape the behavior of routers in the network. These mechanisms enable administrators to selectively advertise or suppress specific routes based on predefined criteria such as route prefixes, route tags, or route attributes. By implementing route filtering, administrators can tailor the routing information exchanged between routers to meet specific network requirements and constraints.

One commonly used route filtering mechanism is the access control list (ACL), which allows administrators to define rules for permitting or denying traffic based on various criteria, including source and destination IP addresses, protocol types, and port numbers. In the context of routing, ACLs can be applied to filter routing updates between routers to control which routes are advertised or accepted.

To implement route filtering using ACLs, administrators can define ACLs to match specific route prefixes or attributes and then apply these ACLs to filter routing updates. For example, to filter routes based on their destination IP addresses, administrators can create an ACL to permit or deny specific IP address ranges and then apply this ACL to filter routing updates using the "distribute-list" command in router configuration mode:

phpCopy code

router ospf <process_ID> distribute-list <ACL_number> <in | out> <interface>

In this command, "<ACL_number>" specifies the number of the ACL configured to filter routes, and "<in | out>" indicates whether the ACL is applied to incoming or outgoing routing updates on the specified interface.

Another route filtering mechanism commonly used in routing protocols such as OSPF and BGP is route maps. Route maps provide a more flexible and granular approach to route filtering compared to ACLs, allowing administrators to define multiple match and set conditions for filtering routes.

To implement route filtering using route maps, administrators can define route maps to match specific route attributes or conditions and then apply these route maps to filter routing updates. For example, to filter OSPF routes based on their route tags, administrators can create a route map to match routes with specific route tags and then apply this route map to filter routing updates using the "distribute-list" command in router configuration mode:

phpCopy code

router ospf <process_ID> distribute-list route-map <route_map_name> <in | out> <interface>

In this command, "<route_map_name>" specifies the name of the route map configured to filter routes.

Route filtering mechanisms can also be used to implement route summarization and aggregation, which involve consolidating multiple contiguous routes into a single summarized route to reduce the size of routing tables and minimize the overhead associated with route advertisement. By summarizing routes, administrators can optimize routing table memory utilization and improve network scalability and efficiency.

To implement route summarization using route filtering mechanisms, administrators can define summary routes and associated subnet masks using route maps or ACLs and then apply these filters to summarize routes. For example, to summarize OSPF routes for networks 192.168.0.0/24 and 192.168.1.0/24 into a single summary route, administrators can create a route map to match these routes and then apply this route map to summarize routes using the "summary-address" command in router configuration mode:

cssCopy code

```
router ospf <process_ID> summary-address
192.168.0.0 255.255.254.0
```

In addition to ACLs and route maps, routing protocols such as BGP also support community-based route filtering, which allows administrators to tag routes with community attributes and then filter routes based on these attributes. Community-based route filtering provides a flexible and scalable mechanism for controlling route propagation and shaping traffic flow in the network.

Overall, route filtering mechanisms are essential tools for network administrators to manage routing information and control the flow of traffic in the network. By leveraging ACLs, route maps, and other filtering techniques, administrators can enforce routing policies, optimize network performance, and enhance network security and stability.

Prefix lists and route maps are essential tools in network routing for implementing route filtering and traffic control policies. These mechanisms allow network administrators to selectively permit or deny routing updates based on specific criteria such as IP address prefixes, AS paths, or route attributes. By leveraging prefix lists and route maps, administrators can customize routing behavior, optimize network performance, and enhance security.

Prefix lists are used to filter routes based on their IP address prefixes. They provide a simple and efficient way to permit or deny routes based on specific prefix lengths or address ranges. To configure a prefix list, administrators define one or more prefix list entries, each specifying a prefix and an action (permit or deny). These entries are then applied to router configuration to filter routing updates.

For example, to create a prefix list to permit routes for the 192.168.0.0/24 and 10.0.0.0/8 networks, administrators can use the following command:

bashCopy code

ip prefix-list ALLOWED_ROUTES seq 10 permit 192.168.0.0/24 ip prefix-list ALLOWED_ROUTES seq 20 permit 10.0.0.0/8

In this command, "seq 10" and "seq 20" specify the sequence numbers for the prefix list entries, "permit" indicates that the specified prefix is permitted, and

"192.168.0.0/24" and "10.0.0.0/8" define the IP address prefixes to be allowed.

Once the prefix list is configured, it can be applied to filter routing updates using routing protocols such as OSPF or BGP. For example, to apply the prefix list to filter OSPF routes on an interface, administrators can use the following command:

kotlinCopy code

```
router ospf 1 distribute-list prefix ALLOWED_ROUTES in interface GigabitEthernet0/0
```

In this command, "distribute-list prefix ALLOWED_ROUTES" specifies that the prefix list named "ALLOWED_ROUTES" should be used to filter OSPF routes, and "in interface GigabitEthernet0/0" indicates that the filtering should be applied on the specified interface.

Route maps, on the other hand, provide more flexibility and granularity in route filtering compared to prefix lists. They allow administrators to define multiple match and set conditions to control route advertisement and propagation. Route maps can match various criteria such as IP address prefixes, AS paths, or route tags and apply different actions based on these criteria.

To configure a route map for route filtering, administrators define a route map entry specifying match and set conditions and actions. These entries are then applied to router configuration to filter routing updates or modify route attributes.

For example, to create a route map to permit routes for the 192.168.0.0/24 network and deny all other routes, administrators can use the following command:

pythonCopy code

```
route-map ALLOWED_ROUTES permit 10 match ip
address prefix-list ALLOWED_PREFIXES route-map
ALLOWED_ROUTES deny 20
```

In this command, "permit 10" and "deny 20" specify the sequence numbers for the route map entries, and "match ip address prefix-list ALLOWED_PREFIXES" specifies the condition to match routes with the specified prefix list.

Once the route map is configured, it can be applied to filter routing updates using routing protocols or redistribute routes between routing protocols. For example, to apply the route map to filter BGP routes, administrators can use the following command:

arduinoCopy code

```
router bgp 65001 neighbor 192.168.1.1 route-map
ALLOWED_ROUTES in
```

In this command, "neighbor 192.168.1.1" specifies the BGP neighbor to which the route map should be applied, and "route-map ALLOWED_ROUTES in" indicates that the route map should be applied to incoming BGP routes.

Prefix lists and route maps are powerful tools for route filtering and traffic control in network routing. By leveraging these mechanisms, administrators can implement fine-grained routing policies to optimize network performance, ensure network security, and meet specific business requirements.

Chapter 7: Multicast Routing Protocols

Multicast communication is a vital aspect of network routing, facilitating efficient data transmission to multiple recipients simultaneously. Unlike unicast communication, where data is sent from one sender to one receiver, multicast allows a sender to transmit data to a group of receivers using a single transmission. This capability is particularly beneficial for applications such as video streaming, online gaming, and audio conferencing, where data needs to be distributed to multiple recipients efficiently.

At the core of multicast communication is the concept of multicast groups, which represent logical channels through which data is transmitted. Each multicast group is identified by a unique IP address from the IPv4 range of 224.0.0.0 to 239.255.255.255. These addresses are reserved specifically for multicast purposes and are not associated with individual devices. Instead, devices interested in receiving data sent to a multicast group join that group by subscribing to its corresponding IP address.

To understand how multicast works in practice, consider the example of streaming live video to multiple users over a network. In this scenario, the video stream is transmitted from a server to a multicast group address, and users interested in watching the stream join the multicast group to receive the video data. By subscribing to the multicast group, users effectively become part of the multicast distribution tree, through which data flows from the sender to the receivers.

In terms of deployment, enabling multicast communication requires support from network infrastructure devices such as routers and switches. Routers play a crucial role in forwarding multicast traffic between different network segments, while switches are responsible for efficiently distributing multicast data within local network segments.

To enable multicast routing on a router, administrators typically configure multicast routing protocols such as Protocol Independent Multicast (PIM) or Multicast Source Discovery Protocol (MSDP). These protocols allow routers to exchange multicast routing information and build multicast distribution trees dynamically. For instance, to enable PIM sparse mode on a router interface, the following command can be used:

kotlinCopy code

interface GigabitEthernet0/1 ip pim sparse-mode

This command instructs the router to enable PIM sparse mode on the specified interface, indicating that the router should forward multicast traffic only when it has receivers interested in receiving data for specific multicast groups.

In addition to enabling multicast routing, administrators may need to configure multicast forwarding and replication mechanisms on switches to ensure efficient delivery of multicast traffic within local network segments. This involves configuring features such as Internet Group Management Protocol (IGMP) snooping, which allows switches to learn which hosts are members of multicast groups and forward multicast traffic only to those hosts.

To enable IGMP snooping on a switch, the following command can be used:

Copy code

ip igmp snooping

This command enables IGMP snooping globally on the switch, allowing it to monitor IGMP messages exchanged between hosts and multicast routers and optimize multicast traffic forwarding accordingly.

Beyond traditional data transmission, multicast has various applications in modern networking environments. For example, multicast is commonly used in audio and video conferencing applications to deliver real-time audio and video streams to multiple participants simultaneously. Similarly, multicast is utilized in content distribution networks (CDNs) to efficiently distribute multimedia content, software updates, and other data to geographically dispersed users.

Overall, multicast communication offers significant advantages in terms of bandwidth efficiency, scalability, and simplicity compared to unicast communication. By leveraging multicast technology, organizations can optimize network resource utilization and deliver high-quality multimedia content and services to a large audience efficiently.

Configuring Protocol Independent Multicast (PIM) is a crucial aspect of enabling multicast routing in network environments. PIM is a family of multicast routing protocols designed to efficiently route multicast traffic across IP networks. Unlike traditional multicast routing protocols such as Distance Vector Multicast Routing Protocol (DVMRP) or Multicast Open Shortest Path First (MOSPF), PIM operates independently of any specific unicast routing protocol, hence the name "Protocol Independent."

To begin configuring PIM on a router, it's essential to understand the different modes in which PIM operates: Dense Mode (PIM-DM), Sparse Mode (PIM-SM), and Sparse-Dense Mode. Dense Mode floods multicast traffic initially and prunes back where there are no receivers. Sparse Mode, on the other hand, relies on explicit join messages from receivers to build the multicast distribution tree. Sparse-Dense Mode is a hybrid mode that combines aspects of both dense and sparse modes, enabling routers to operate in dense mode until explicit join messages are received.

To enable PIM on an interface in Sparse Mode, the following command can be used:

kotlinCopy code

interface GigabitEthernet0/1 ip pim sparse-mode

This command instructs the router to enable PIM Sparse Mode on the specified interface, indicating that the router should forward multicast traffic only when it has receivers interested in receiving data for specific multicast groups. Sparse mode is typically used in networks with sparse receiver populations or when conserving network bandwidth is a priority.

In addition to enabling PIM on individual interfaces, routers participating in multicast routing must be configured with a rendezvous point (RP) to facilitate the distribution of multicast traffic. The RP acts as a central point for the rendezvous of sources and receivers in a multicast group and is responsible for maintaining group membership information.

To configure a router as a rendezvous point (RP) for PIM Sparse Mode, the following command can be used:

cssCopy code

```
ip pim rp-address <RP-ADDRESS>
```

This command specifies the IP address of the router that will serve as the rendezvous point for multicast groups. It's important to ensure that routers participating in PIM Sparse Mode have consistent RP configurations to ensure proper multicast traffic distribution.

Furthermore, PIM Sparse Mode relies on a mechanism called the Bootstrap Router (BSR) to distribute RP information dynamically within the network. The BSR is responsible for electing candidate Rendezvous Point (RP) routers and propagating RP mapping information to other routers in the network.

To enable BSR functionality on a router, the following command can be used:

csharpCopy code

```
ip pim bsr-candidate <interface>
```

This command configures the router as a candidate Bootstrap Router (BSR), allowing it to participate in the election process and propagate RP mapping information to other routers in the network.

Beyond basic configuration, it's essential to monitor and troubleshoot PIM operation to ensure optimal multicast routing performance. This involves regularly inspecting multicast routing tables, interface states, and RP information to identify any issues that may affect multicast traffic distribution.

To view PIM routing information on a Cisco router, the following command can be used:

sqlCopy code

show ip mroute

This command displays the multicast routing table, which contains information about multicast group memberships, incoming and outgoing interfaces, and the status of multicast routes.

In summary, configuring PIM is a critical step in enabling multicast routing in network environments. By understanding the different modes of operation, configuring routers with appropriate PIM modes and RP configurations, and monitoring PIM operation, network administrators can ensure efficient multicast traffic distribution and optimal network performance.

Chapter 8: MPLS (Multiprotocol Label Switching) Fundamentals

Multiprotocol Label Switching (MPLS) is a versatile and powerful technique used in modern networking to improve the efficiency and performance of packet-switched networks. At its core, MPLS is an encapsulation mechanism that enables the forwarding of data packets based on labels rather than traditional IP routing tables. This architecture introduces several key components that work together to facilitate efficient packet forwarding and traffic engineering within MPLS networks.

One of the fundamental components of MPLS architecture is the Label Switch Router (LSR). LSRs are responsible for forwarding packets based on the labels assigned to them. These labels are added to packets as they enter the MPLS network and are used by LSRs to determine the next hop for packet forwarding. LSRs maintain Label Forwarding Information Bases (LFIBs), which contain mappings of incoming labels to outgoing interfaces and labels.

To view the LFIB on a Cisco router, the following command can be used:

sqlCopy code

```
show mpls forwarding-table
```

This command displays the LFIB, showing the mappings of incoming labels to outgoing interfaces and labels, along with other relevant information.

Another crucial component of MPLS architecture is the Label Edge Router (LER). LERs sit at the edge of MPLS networks and are responsible for imposing and removing MPLS labels on packets as they enter and exit the MPLS domain, respectively. LERs mark packets with MPLS labels based on predetermined criteria, such as destination IP address, before forwarding them into the MPLS network. Similarly, they remove MPLS labels from packets before forwarding them outside the MPLS domain.

To configure an interface as a Label Edge Router (LER) on a Cisco router, the following command can be used:
kotlinCopy code

```
interface GigabitEthernet0/0 mpls ip
```

This command enables MPLS on the specified interface, allowing the router to impose MPLS labels on outgoing packets.

MPLS networks also include Label Distribution Protocol (LDP) routers, which are responsible for distributing labels to other routers in the MPLS domain. LDP routers use a signaling protocol to exchange label information and build Label Information Bases (LIBs), which contain mappings of network prefixes to labels. These mappings are then used by LSRs to forward packets based on the labels assigned by LDP routers.

To view the Label Information Base (LIB) on a Cisco router, the following command can be used:
sqlCopy code

```
show mpls ldp bindings
```

This command displays the mappings between network prefixes and labels learned through LDP signaling.

In addition to LDP, MPLS networks can utilize other label distribution protocols, such as Resource Reservation Protocol - Traffic Engineering (RSVP-TE), which allows for more granular control over traffic engineering and Quality of Service (QoS) in MPLS networks. RSVP-TE enables routers to establish Label Switched Paths (LSPs) with specific bandwidth and QoS requirements, providing a mechanism for optimizing network resource utilization and meeting service level agreements (SLAs).

To configure RSVP-TE on a Cisco router, the following commands can be used:

Copy code

```
mpls traffic-eng tunnels
```

This command enables MPLS Traffic Engineering globally on the router.

csharpCopy code

```
interface Tunnel0 mpls traffic-eng tunnel destination
<destination-address>
```

This command creates an MPLS Traffic Engineering tunnel interface and specifies the destination address of the tunnel.

Overall, MPLS architecture comprises various components, including LSRs, LERs, and label distribution protocols like LDP and RSVP-TE, working together to enable efficient packet forwarding and traffic engineering in MPLS networks. By understanding the roles and functions of these components, network administrators can design and deploy MPLS networks that meet the requirements of modern applications and services.

MPLS Label Distribution Protocol (LDP) is a crucial component of MPLS networks, responsible for distributing labels to routers within the MPLS domain to facilitate label-switched packet forwarding. Configuring LDP involves several steps and commands to enable label distribution and establish label-switched paths (LSPs) across the network.

The first step in configuring LDP is to enable MPLS on the interfaces participating in MPLS forwarding. This can be achieved using the 'mpls ip' command under the interface configuration mode. For example, to enable MPLS on a specific interface on a Cisco router, you would enter the following command:

kotlinCopy code

interface GigabitEthernet0/0 mpls ip

This command instructs the router to use MPLS for forwarding IP packets on the specified interface.

Once MPLS is enabled on the interfaces, the next step is to configure the LDP protocol globally on the router. This is done using the 'mpls ldp router-id' command, which assigns a unique router ID to the router for LDP neighborship purposes. The router ID can be an IP address or a hostname. Here's an example of how to configure the router ID:

pythonCopy code

mpls ldp router-id <router-id>

Replace '<router-id>' with the desired identifier for the router.

After configuring the router ID, LDP can be enabled globally on the router using the 'mpls ldp enable' command. This command activates the LDP process on the router, allowing it to participate in label distribution with neighboring routers:

bashCopy code

```
mpls ldp enable
```

With LDP enabled, the router will start exchanging label information with neighboring routers using the LDP protocol. To verify the status of LDP neighborships and the label bindings learned from neighboring routers, the 'show mpls ldp neighbor' and 'show mpls ldp bindings' commands can be used, respectively:

sqlCopy code

```
show mpls ldp neighbor show mpls ldp bindings
```

These commands provide information about the LDP neighbors of the router and the label bindings received from them.

In addition to the basic LDP configuration, there are advanced options available for fine-tuning the behavior of LDP. For example, administrators can configure LDP session protection to maintain label bindings during router restarts or interface flaps. This can be achieved using the 'mpls ldp session protection' command:

Copy code

```
mpls ldp session protection
```

This command enables LDP session protection on the router, ensuring that label bindings remain intact during transient network events.

Furthermore, administrators can configure LDP authentication to secure LDP neighborships and prevent unauthorized routers from participating in label distribution. LDP authentication requires configuring a shared secret between neighboring routers using the 'mpls ldp neighbor <neighbor-ip> password <password>' command:

phpCopy code

mpls ldp neighbor <neighbor-ip> password <password>

Replace '<neighbor-ip>' with the IP address of the neighboring router and '<password>' with the shared secret.

Overall, configuring MPLS Label Distribution Protocol (LDP) involves enabling MPLS on interfaces, configuring the router ID, enabling LDP globally, and optionally configuring advanced features like session protection and authentication. By following these steps and commands, administrators can deploy LDP in MPLS networks to facilitate efficient label distribution and label-switched packet forwarding.

Chapter 9: IPv6 Routing Considerations

IPv6, the next-generation Internet Protocol, is designed to address the limitations of IPv4 and provide a vast address space to accommodate the growing number of devices connected to the internet. One of the fundamental aspects of IPv6 is its addressing scheme, which differs significantly from IPv4. IPv6 addresses are 128 bits long, allowing for a staggering number of unique addresses compared to the 32-bit addresses of IPv4. To deploy IPv6 in a network, administrators need to understand IPv6 addressing and routing protocols, which play a crucial role in IPv6 network communication.

IPv6 addressing follows a hierarchical structure, similar to IPv4, but with some notable differences. IPv6 addresses are represented in hexadecimal notation and are divided into multiple sections separated by colons. One of the key features of IPv6 addressing is the inclusion of subnet prefixes directly in the address itself, eliminating the need for subnet masks. For example, an IPv6 address might look like '2001:0db8:85a3:0000:0000:8a2e:0370:7334', where the first 64 bits represent the network prefix, and the remaining 64 bits identify the specific host within the network.

To configure IPv6 addressing on a router interface, the 'ipv6 address' command is used. For instance, to

assign the IPv6 address '2001:0db8::1/64' to an interface, the following command would be used:
kotlinCopy code

```
interface      GigabitEthernet0/0      ipv6      address
2001:0db8::1/64
```

This command assigns the specified IPv6 address and prefix length to the interface, enabling IPv6 communication on that interface.

In addition to static IPv6 addressing, IPv6 also supports dynamic address assignment through protocols like Stateless Address Autoconfiguration (SLAAC) and Dynamic Host Configuration Protocol version 6 (DHCPv6). SLAAC allows IPv6 hosts to configure their own addresses by combining network prefixes received from routers with their interface identifiers. On the other hand, DHCPv6 provides a centralized method for distributing IPv6 addresses and other configuration parameters to hosts.

Routing in IPv6 networks is facilitated by routing protocols specifically designed for IPv6, such as Routing Information Protocol next generation (RIPng), OSPF version 3 (OSPFv3), and Enhanced Interior Gateway Routing Protocol for IPv6 (EIGRPv6). These protocols operate similarly to their IPv4 counterparts but have been updated to support IPv6 addressing and network structures.

To configure IPv6 routing protocols, administrators use commands specific to each protocol. For example, to enable OSPFv3 on a router, the following commands would be used:

phpCopy code
ipv6 unicast-routing router ospf 1 network <network-prefix> <wildcard-mask> area <area-id>

Replace '<network-prefix>' with the IPv6 network prefix, '<wildcard-mask>' with the wildcard mask, and '<area-id>' with the OSPF area identifier.

Similarly, EIGRPv6 configuration involves enabling IPv6 routing and configuring the EIGRP process:

phpCopy code
ipv6 unicast-routing ipv6 router eigrp <as-number> network <network-prefix>

Replace '<as-number>' with the EIGRP autonomous system number and '<network-prefix>' with the IPv6 network prefix to be advertised by EIGRP.

As IPv6 adoption continues to grow, understanding IPv6 addressing and routing protocols becomes increasingly important for network administrators. By familiarizing themselves with IPv6 addressing schemes and configuring routing protocols tailored for IPv6, administrators can ensure the smooth operation of IPv6 networks and pave the way for the future of internet connectivity.

Transitioning to IPv6 routing in existing networks is a critical step in adapting to the evolving landscape of internet protocols. With the exhaustion of IPv4 addresses and the increasing adoption of IPv6, organizations must plan and execute a smooth migration strategy to ensure uninterrupted connectivity for their networks. IPv6 routing introduces several considerations and challenges, but with careful planning and implementation, organizations can successfully integrate IPv6 into their existing infrastructure.

The first step in transitioning to IPv6 routing is to assess the current network topology and infrastructure. This involves identifying existing IPv4 routing protocols, such as OSPF, EIGRP, or BGP, and evaluating their compatibility with IPv6. While some routing protocols support both IPv4 and IPv6 simultaneously, others may require updates or replacements to support IPv6 routing.

To determine the readiness of the network for IPv6 routing, administrators can use various network assessment tools and commands to gather information about the existing routing configuration. For example, the 'show ip route' command in Cisco IOS can be used to display the IPv4 routing table, while the 'show ipv6 route' command reveals the IPv6 routing table. This allows administrators to compare the routing information for IPv4 and IPv6 and identify any discrepancies or missing routes.

Once the network assessment is complete, the next step is to plan the IPv6 addressing scheme and topology. Unlike IPv4, which often relies on NAT (Network Address Translation) to conserve address space, IPv6 provides an abundance of globally unique addresses, allowing for a more straightforward addressing scheme. However, designing an efficient

IPv6 addressing plan requires careful consideration of subnetting, address allocation, and routing hierarchy.

One common approach to IPv6 addressing is to assign a /64 subnet to each LAN segment, following the recommendations outlined in RFC 4291. This provides ample address space for host devices while simplifying address assignment and routing. Additionally, organizations may choose to adopt IPv6 address assignment methods such as SLAAC (Stateless Address Autoconfiguration) or DHCPv6 (Dynamic Host Configuration Protocol version 6) to automate the configuration process for IPv6 hosts.

With the addressing plan in place, the next step is to configure IPv6 routing protocols on network devices. As mentioned earlier, many routing protocols support both IPv4 and IPv6 simultaneously, allowing for a phased migration approach. For example, OSPFv3 (OSPF version 3) and EIGRPv6 (Enhanced Interior Gateway Routing Protocol for IPv6) are commonly used in IPv6 networks and can be configured alongside their IPv4 counterparts.

To enable IPv6 routing protocols, administrators use commands similar to their IPv4 counterparts, with slight modifications for IPv6 configuration. For instance, to configure OSPFv3 on a Cisco router, the following commands are used:

phpCopy code

```
ipv6 unicast-routing ipv6 router ospf <process-id>
network <network-prefix> area <area-id>
```

Replace '<process-id>' with the OSPF process identifier, '<network-prefix>' with the IPv6 network prefix to be advertised by OSPF, and '<area-id>' with the OSPF area identifier.

Similarly, EIGRPv6 configuration involves enabling IPv6 routing and configuring the EIGRP process:

phpCopy code

```
ipv6 unicast-routing ipv6 router eigrp <as-number>
network <network-prefix>
```

Replace '<as-number>' with the EIGRP autonomous system number and '<network-prefix>' with the IPv6 network prefix to be advertised by EIGRP.

As part of the transition process, administrators must also ensure interoperability between IPv4 and IPv6 networks. This includes configuring dual-stack routing, where both IPv4 and IPv6 protocols are enabled on network devices to facilitate communication between IPv4 and IPv6 hosts. Dual-stack routing allows for a gradual migration of services and applications to IPv6 while maintaining compatibility with existing IPv4 infrastructure.

In addition to routing protocols, administrators must also consider other network services and protocols that may require IPv6 support, such as DNS (Domain Name System), DHCPv6, and NTP (Network Time Protocol). Configuring these services to support IPv6 ensures seamless operation in an IPv6-enabled environment.

Throughout the transition process, thorough testing and validation are essential to identify and address any issues or compatibility issues that may arise. Network monitoring tools and diagnostic commands can help administrators monitor the performance and stability of the IPv6 network and troubleshoot any connectivity or routing issues.

In summary, transitioning to IPv6 routing in existing networks is a complex but necessary undertaking in today's digital landscape. By carefully planning and executing a migration strategy, organizations can embrace the benefits of IPv6, including a larger address space, improved security, and enhanced network performance, while ensuring continuity of service for their users and applications.

Chapter 10: Network Scalability and Performance Optimization

Scaling network infrastructure is a critical aspect of network management and design, especially in environments experiencing growth or increased demands on network resources. As organizations expand their operations, the need for a scalable and reliable network infrastructure becomes paramount to accommodate the growing number of users, devices, and services accessing the network. Scaling network infrastructure involves implementing strategies and technologies to ensure that the network can handle increased traffic volumes, maintain performance, and support future growth without sacrificing reliability or security.

One fundamental aspect of scaling network infrastructure is the design of a robust and resilient network architecture. This includes creating a hierarchical network design that separates network traffic into different layers, such as access, distribution, and core layers. By segmenting the network into distinct layers, organizations can improve scalability, simplify network management, and enhance performance.

A common approach to scaling network infrastructure is to deploy modular and scalable hardware components, such as routers, switches, and firewalls. These devices should support features like high port densities, modular expansion slots, and redundant power supplies to accommodate future growth and provide resilience against hardware failures. For example, Cisco Catalyst switches offer various models with different port densities and modular expansion options to scale network capacity as needed.

In addition to hardware scalability, organizations must also consider the scalability of network services and protocols. For example, dynamic routing protocols like OSPF and BGP offer scalability features such as route summarization, route aggregation, and hierarchical routing to optimize routing table size and reduce overhead. By implementing these scalability features, organizations can ensure efficient routing and minimize the impact of routing updates on network performance.

Another critical aspect of scaling network infrastructure is optimizing network bandwidth utilization and performance. This involves implementing technologies like Quality of Service (QoS) and traffic engineering to prioritize and manage network traffic effectively. QoS mechanisms allow organizations to prioritize critical traffic, such as voice and video, over less time-sensitive data traffic to ensure optimal performance for real-time applications. Additionally, traffic engineering techniques like traffic shaping and load balancing help distribute network traffic evenly across available paths to prevent congestion and optimize network performance.

To deploy QoS and traffic engineering in a network, administrators can use CLI commands to configure policies and parameters on network devices. For example, on Cisco routers and switches, administrators can use commands like 'class-map' and 'policy-map' to define traffic classes and apply QoS policies to prioritize or shape traffic based on predefined criteria. Similarly, traffic engineering protocols like RSVP (Resource Reservation Protocol) can be configured using commands like 'mpls traffic-eng' to set up label-switched paths (LSPs) and control traffic flows across the network.

Scaling network infrastructure also involves implementing redundancy and high availability mechanisms to minimize the impact of hardware failures or network outages. This includes deploying redundant links, devices, and services to ensure continuous operation and seamless failover in the event of a failure. For example, organizations can implement technologies like Virtual Router Redundancy Protocol (VRRP) or Hot Standby Router Protocol (HSRP) to provide redundancy for router gateways and ensure uninterrupted connectivity for end users.

Furthermore, organizations can leverage technologies like virtualization and cloud computing to scale network infrastructure more efficiently and cost-effectively. Virtualization allows organizations to consolidate network services and resources onto fewer physical devices, reducing hardware costs and simplifying management. Cloud computing, on the other hand, enables organizations to offload resource-intensive tasks and services to cloud providers, allowing for elastic scaling of network infrastructure based on demand.

In summary, scaling network infrastructure is essential for meeting the growing demands of modern organizations and ensuring optimal performance, reliability, and security of the network. By implementing scalable network designs, deploying modular hardware components, optimizing bandwidth utilization, and leveraging technologies like virtualization and cloud computing, organizations can effectively scale their network infrastructure to accommodate growth and adapt to changing business requirements.

Performance optimization techniques and best practices play a crucial role in ensuring the efficiency and reliability of network infrastructure, especially in today's high-demand environments where speed and responsiveness are paramount. These techniques encompass a range of strategies and methodologies aimed at maximizing the performance of network devices, applications, and services while minimizing latency, packet loss, and other performance bottlenecks.

One fundamental aspect of performance optimization is proactive monitoring and analysis of network traffic and device metrics. By continuously monitoring key performance indicators (KPIs) such as bandwidth utilization, latency, and packet loss rates, network administrators can identify potential issues and areas for improvement before they impact user experience. CLI commands such as 'show interfaces' and 'show processes cpu' on Cisco devices provide real-time insights into interface statistics and CPU utilization, enabling administrators to diagnose performance issues and take corrective actions promptly.

Another essential technique for performance optimization is traffic prioritization and Quality of Service (QoS) management. QoS allows administrators to prioritize critical traffic types, such as voice or video, over less time-sensitive data traffic to ensure optimal performance for latency-sensitive applications. By configuring QoS policies using CLI commands like 'class-map' and 'policy-map', administrators can classify, mark, and prioritize traffic based on predefined criteria, ensuring that mission-critical applications receive sufficient bandwidth and network resources.

Additionally, performance optimization involves optimizing network protocols and configurations to minimize overhead and maximize efficiency. For example, tuning routing protocols such as OSPF or BGP to reduce convergence times and optimize routing table sizes can improve overall network performance. CLI commands like 'router ospf' or 'router bgp' allow administrators to adjust parameters such as hello timers, dead intervals, and route summarization to optimize protocol operation and reduce network overhead.

Another critical aspect of performance optimization is the efficient utilization of network hardware resources. This includes optimizing device configurations, such as adjusting buffer sizes, tuning forwarding tables, and enabling hardware acceleration features, to maximize device throughput and minimize packet processing latency. CLI commands like 'hardware queue' and 'buffer tuning' allow administrators to fine-tune device settings to optimize performance based on specific workload requirements.

Furthermore, implementing caching and content delivery mechanisms can significantly improve application performance and reduce bandwidth consumption by serving frequently accessed content from local caches rather than fetching it from remote servers. Content caching solutions like Squid or NGINX can be deployed on proxy servers or content delivery networks (CDNs) to cache web content, images, and multimedia files, reducing latency and improving user experience.

Moreover, performance optimization involves optimizing network security mechanisms to minimize the impact on network performance while ensuring robust protection against security threats. This includes implementing efficient firewall rules, intrusion detection and prevention systems (IDPS), and encryption protocols to secure network traffic without introducing significant overhead. CLI commands like 'access-list' and 'crypto map' allow administrators to configure firewall rules and VPN tunnels to enforce security policies while minimizing performance impact.

Additionally, optimizing application and server performance is essential for ensuring optimal network performance. Techniques such as application profiling, code optimization, and server load balancing can help distribute workload efficiently across server clusters and prevent resource contention issues. CLI commands like 'show processes' and 'show server farm' on Cisco devices provide visibility into server performance metrics and load balancing configurations, enabling administrators to monitor and optimize application performance effectively.

Furthermore, network segmentation and traffic isolation can help improve performance by reducing congestion and isolating traffic flows between different network segments or user groups. Techniques such as VLAN segmentation, subnetting, and access control lists (ACLs) can be used to segment traffic and enforce traffic policies based on specific criteria. CLI commands like 'vlan' and 'access-list' allow administrators to create VLANs and apply traffic filtering policies to control traffic flows and improve performance.

In summary, performance optimization techniques and best practices are essential for maximizing the efficiency, reliability, and responsiveness of network infrastructure in today's dynamic and demanding environments. By proactively monitoring network performance, optimizing network protocols and configurations, prioritizing critical traffic, and optimizing hardware resources, administrators can ensure optimal performance and user experience while minimizing latency, packet loss, and other performance bottlenecks.

BOOK 4
TROUBLESHOOTING MASTERY
EXPERT SOLUTIONS FOR RESOLVING NETWORK
CHALLENGES

ROB BOTWRIGHT

problems with network protocols and applications typically occur at the higher layers.

Another troubleshooting approach is the divide-and-conquer method, which involves isolating the problem by systematically testing different components of the network. This approach helps identify the root cause of the issue by eliminating potential causes one by one until the problem is resolved. For example, if users are experiencing slow internet connectivity, administrators can start by testing the connection to the internet service provider (ISP) to determine if the issue is related to external connectivity. If the connection to the ISP is stable, administrators can then test internal network components such as routers, switches, and firewalls to identify the source of the problem.

Moreover, network administrators often rely on troubleshooting tools and utilities to diagnose and resolve network issues. These tools include network analyzers, packet sniffers, and protocol analyzers, which capture and analyze network traffic to identify anomalies and protocol violations. For example, Wireshark is a popular packet analyzer that allows administrators to capture and inspect network packets in real-time, helping identify network errors, performance issues, and security threats. Additionally, CLI commands such as 'ping', 'traceroute', and 'netstat' provide valuable diagnostic information about network connectivity, latency, and device status, helping administrators pinpoint the source of network problems.

Furthermore, effective troubleshooting requires a good understanding of common network issues and their underlying causes. This includes issues such as network congestion, bandwidth saturation, broadcast storms, and network misconfigurations, which can impact network performance and stability. By familiarizing themselves with common network problems, administrators can quickly recognize symptoms and apply appropriate troubleshooting techniques to resolve them. CLI commands such as 'show interface counters' and 'show processes cpu' can be used to monitor network utilization and identify potential sources of congestion or performance degradation.

In addition to technical troubleshooting skills, effective communication and collaboration are essential for successful problem resolution. In complex network environments, multiple teams and stakeholders may be involved in diagnosing and resolving issues. Therefore, effective communication and coordination between teams, as well as documenting troubleshooting steps and outcomes, are essential for efficient problem resolution. CLI commands such as 'show log' and 'debug' provide detailed logs and debugging information that can be shared with other team members to facilitate collaboration.

Moreover, network documentation and configuration management are critical for effective troubleshooting. Maintaining up-to-date documentation of network topology, device configurations, and network policies helps administrators quickly identify potential sources of problems and roll back changes if necessary.

Configuration management tools such as Ansible and Puppet automate the deployment and management of network configurations, ensuring consistency and reducing the risk of misconfigurations that can lead to network issues.

In summary, troubleshooting network issues requires a systematic approach, effective use of troubleshooting tools and utilities, and good communication and collaboration skills. By following established troubleshooting methodologies, leveraging CLI commands and specialized troubleshooting tools, and working closely with other team members, network administrators can quickly identify and resolve network problems, ensuring optimal network performance and reliability.

Chapter 2: Analyzing Network Traffic with Packet Capture Tools

Packet capture, also known as network sniffing, is a fundamental technique used in network troubleshooting, analysis, and security monitoring. It involves capturing and analyzing the data packets that traverse a network segment to gain insight into network traffic patterns, diagnose connectivity issues, identify performance bottlenecks, and detect security threats. Packet capture is often performed using specialized software tools called packet analyzers or network protocol analyzers, which capture, decode, and display the contents of network packets in real-time or from packet capture files.

One of the most widely used packet capture tools is Wireshark, a free and open-source packet analyzer that runs on various operating systems including Windows, macOS, and Linux. Wireshark provides a graphical user interface (GUI) for capturing and analyzing network packets, making it accessible to both novice and experienced users. To capture packets using Wireshark, users can simply select the network interface they want to monitor and start a capture session. Wireshark captures packets in promiscuous mode, meaning it captures all packets on the network segment, including those not addressed to the capturing device.

Another popular packet capture tool is tcpdump, a command-line packet analyzer available on Unix-like operating systems such as Linux and macOS. Tcpdump provides a powerful command-line interface for capturing and analyzing network packets, making it a favorite among experienced system administrators and network engineers. To capture packets using tcpdump, users can specify various filtering criteria such as source and destination IP addresses, TCP/UDP ports, packet size, and protocol type. For example, the following command captures all packets on the network interface eth0 and writes them to a file named capture.pcap:

bashCopy code

```
tcpdump -i eth0 -w capture.pcap
```

Packet capture is useful for diagnosing a wide range of network issues, including connectivity problems, performance degradation, and security breaches. For example, if users report slow internet access, network administrators can use packet capture to analyze the traffic patterns and identify the source of the slowdown. By inspecting the captured packets, administrators can determine if the slowness is caused by excessive network traffic, bandwidth saturation, or network misconfigurations.

Packet capture is also valuable for detecting and investigating security incidents such as network intrusions, malware infections, and denial-of-service (DoS) attacks. By monitoring network traffic in real-time or reviewing packet capture files, security analysts can identify suspicious or malicious activities such as unauthorized access attempts, data exfiltration, and communication with known malicious domains. For example, if an organization's firewall detects an intrusion attempt, security analysts can use packet capture to analyze the network traffic associated with the attack and determine the extent of the breach.

Moreover, packet capture is essential for troubleshooting protocol-level issues such as TCP/IP errors, packet loss, and retransmissions. By examining the contents of captured packets, network engineers can diagnose protocol violations, identify misconfigured devices, and troubleshoot interoperability issues between different network components. For example, if a client application fails to establish a TCP connection with a server, network engineers can use packet capture to analyze the TCP handshake process and identify any anomalies or errors.

In addition to troubleshooting and security monitoring, packet capture is also valuable for network performance optimization and capacity planning. By analyzing network traffic patterns over time, network administrators can identify peak usage periods, bandwidth-intensive applications, and potential scalability issues. This information can be used to optimize network resources, upgrade infrastructure components, and allocate bandwidth more efficiently. For example, if packet capture reveals that a particular application generates a significant amount of network traffic during peak hours, administrators can prioritize traffic for that application or allocate additional bandwidth to accommodate the increased demand.

Furthermore, packet capture is an essential tool for network forensics and incident response, enabling organizations to reconstruct and analyze network activities during security incidents or data breaches. By capturing and preserving network packets associated with a security incident, forensic analysts can perform detailed investigations to determine the cause of the incident, identify the attackers, and assess the impact on the organization's systems and data. Packet capture can provide valuable evidence for legal proceedings, regulatory compliance, and internal investigations, helping organizations understand how an incident occurred and take steps to prevent future occurrences.

In summary, packet capture is a fundamental technique for network troubleshooting, analysis, and security monitoring. By capturing and analyzing network packets, administrators can diagnose connectivity issues, identify performance bottlenecks, detect security threats, and optimize network performance. Whether performed using graphical packet analyzers like Wireshark or command-line tools like tcpdump, packet capture provides valuable insights into network traffic patterns, enabling organizations to maintain the security, reliability, and efficiency of their networks.

Packet analysis is a crucial skill for network administrators and engineers, enabling them to diagnose and resolve various network issues effectively. It involves examining the contents of network packets to identify anomalies, pinpoint the root cause of problems, and optimize network performance. Packet analysis techniques encompass a wide range of methods and tools, including packet capture, protocol analysis, traffic filtering, and statistical analysis.

One of the primary packet analysis techniques is packet capture, which involves capturing and storing network packets for analysis. Packet capture allows administrators to inspect the traffic traversing their network in real-time or retrospectively. Wireshark, a popular packet analysis tool, provides a comprehensive graphical interface for capturing and analyzing packets. With Wireshark, administrators can capture packets on specific network interfaces or apply filters to capture only packets matching certain criteria.

Once packets are captured, protocol analysis becomes essential for understanding the behavior of network protocols and identifying any deviations from expected norms. Protocol analysis involves examining the headers and payloads of captured packets to analyze protocol interactions and detect protocol-level issues. Wireshark's packet dissection feature enables administrators to dissect and analyze various network protocols, including TCP, UDP, ICMP, HTTP, DNS, and more. By analyzing protocol headers and payloads, administrators can diagnose protocol errors, performance bottlenecks, and compatibility issues.

Traffic filtering is another critical packet analysis technique used to focus on specific types of traffic or isolate packets related to a particular issue. By applying filters to captured packets, administrators can narrow down their analysis to relevant traffic patterns and discard irrelevant packets. Wireshark supports flexible traffic filtering capabilities, allowing administrators to create filters based on various criteria such as IP addresses, port numbers, protocol types, packet lengths, and more. For example, administrators can use Wireshark's display filters to show only packets exchanged between specific IP addresses or packets containing certain keywords in their payloads.

Statistical analysis is a powerful packet analysis technique used to extract meaningful insights from large volumes of packet data. By analyzing packet statistics, administrators can identify trends, patterns, and anomalies in network traffic, enabling them to make informed decisions about network optimization and troubleshooting. Wireshark provides statistical analysis features such as packet counters, protocol distribution charts, conversation statistics, and endpoint statistics. Administrators can use these features to analyze network traffic patterns, identify top talkers, detect abnormal behavior, and assess network performance metrics.

Furthermore, packet analysis techniques can be combined with other network troubleshooting methodologies to enhance their effectiveness. For example, when troubleshooting connectivity issues, administrators can use packet capture to capture packets exchanged between a client and server, protocol analysis to examine the TCP handshake process, traffic filtering to isolate packets related to the connection attempt, and statistical analysis to identify packet loss or latency issues.

In addition to Wireshark, there are other packet analysis tools available that offer similar capabilities for network troubleshooting and analysis. Tcpdump, a command-line packet analyzer, provides powerful packet capture and filtering capabilities for Unix-like operating systems. Tshark, the command-line counterpart of Wireshark, offers similar packet analysis features and can be used for automated or scripted packet analysis tasks.

Overall, packet analysis techniques play a crucial role in network troubleshooting, enabling administrators to diagnose and resolve various network issues effectively. By capturing, dissecting, filtering, and analyzing network packets, administrators can gain valuable insights into network traffic patterns, protocol interactions, and performance metrics, helping them maintain the security, reliability, and efficiency of their networks.

Chapter 3: Diagnosing Connectivity Issues: Layer 1 and Layer 2 Problems

Layer 1 troubleshooting, focusing on physical layer issues, constitutes a foundational aspect of network troubleshooting. At this layer, problems typically involve physical cabling, connectors, and hardware components. One of the most common physical layer issues is cable faults, which can result from damaged cables, loose connections, or improper termination. To diagnose cable faults, network administrators often use cable testers, such as the cable test feature available on Cisco switches. By connecting the cable tester to both ends of the cable, administrators can perform continuity tests to check for breaks or shorts in the cable.

Another prevalent physical layer issue is connector problems, which can arise from damaged or corroded connectors. To address connector issues, administrators may inspect connectors visually for signs of damage or corrosion. Additionally, they can use a cable certifier, such as Fluke Networks' CableIQ, to measure connector quality and verify compliance with industry standards. By conducting connector tests, administrators can ensure that connectors meet performance requirements and minimize signal degradation.

Moreover, issues related to cable length and signal attenuation can impact network performance at the physical layer. Ethernet cables have maximum length limits based on the cable type and network speed. Exceeding these limits can result in signal degradation and data transmission errors. To troubleshoot cable length issues, administrators can use a time domain reflectometer (TDR) to measure cable length and identify any discrepancies between the actual and expected lengths. Additionally, they can use CLI commands like "show interfaces" on Cisco switches to monitor signal strength and detect potential attenuation problems.

Environmental factors, such as electromagnetic interference (EMI) and radio frequency interference (RFI), can also cause physical layer issues by disrupting signal transmission. EMI and RFI sources include power cables, fluorescent lights, electric motors, and wireless devices. To mitigate interference problems, administrators can relocate affected cables away from potential sources of interference or use shielded cables to reduce susceptibility to external noise. Furthermore, they can use spectrum analyzers to identify and analyze electromagnetic interference patterns in the environment.

Additionally, power-related issues, such as power surges, voltage fluctuations, and ground loops, can impact network equipment and cause physical layer problems. Unstable power sources can damage network devices or lead to erratic behavior. To address power-related issues, administrators can use uninterruptible power supplies (UPS) to provide backup power during outages and stabilize voltage levels. Moreover, they can use power monitoring tools to track power consumption and detect abnormal power fluctuations.

Furthermore, physical layer issues can also stem from hardware failures, such as malfunctioning network interface cards (NICs), switches, or routers. Hardware failures can manifest as connectivity issues, packet loss, or device unresponsiveness. To troubleshoot hardware problems, administrators can perform diagnostic tests, such as loopback tests, to isolate faulty components. Additionally, they can use hardware diagnostic commands, such as "show interfaces" and "show hardware," to identify hardware errors or failures on network devices.

In summary, physical layer troubleshooting is essential for maintaining the reliability and performance of network infrastructure. By identifying and resolving physical layer issues promptly, administrators can ensure smooth network operation and minimize downtime. Through a combination of visual inspection, cable testing, diagnostic tools, and CLI commands, administrators can effectively diagnose and address physical layer problems, ensuring the integrity of the network infrastructure.

Layer 2 troubleshooting involves addressing data link layer problems, which primarily occur between adjacent network devices and are often related to Ethernet frames and MAC addresses. One common issue at this layer is frame collisions, where two devices attempt to transmit data simultaneously, causing packet loss and degraded network performance. Administrators can diagnose and mitigate collisions using the "show interfaces" command on Cisco switches to monitor collision counts and identify interfaces experiencing high collision rates. Additionally, implementing full-duplex Ethernet connections and segmenting networks into smaller collision domains can help minimize collisions and improve network reliability.

Another prevalent problem at the data link layer is duplex mismatch, which occurs when connected devices have mismatched duplex settings, leading to performance issues and intermittent connectivity problems. Administrators can verify and correct duplex settings using the "show interfaces" command to ensure consistent settings across all interconnected devices. Additionally, configuring interfaces to auto-negotiate duplex settings can prevent duplex mismatch issues by allowing devices to negotiate optimal settings dynamically.

Moreover, spanning tree protocol (STP) issues can impact network stability and lead to broadcast storms or network loops. STP problems may arise from misconfigurations, such as incorrect bridge priorities or disabled STP instances. Administrators can diagnose STP issues using the "show spanning-tree" command to view STP topology information and identify root bridge elections, designated ports, and blocked ports. By analyzing STP output, administrators can identify misconfigurations and take corrective actions, such as adjusting bridge priorities or enabling STP on affected interfaces.

Additionally, MAC address table inconsistencies can cause forwarding problems and disrupt communication between devices on the same network segment. MAC address table inconsistencies may result from stale entries, duplicate MAC addresses, or incorrect port mappings. Administrators can use the "show mac address-table" command on Cisco switches to display the MAC address table contents and verify the accuracy of MAC address mappings. Furthermore, periodically clearing the MAC address table or configuring aging timers can help prevent stale entries and maintain table integrity.

Furthermore, VLAN-related issues, such as VLAN mismatch or VLAN configuration errors, can cause connectivity problems and isolate devices from the network. Administrators can use the "show vlan" command to view VLAN configurations and verify consistency across interconnected switches. Additionally, troubleshooting VLAN trunking issues involves verifying trunk configurations, native VLAN settings, and allowed VLAN lists using the "show interfaces trunk" command. By ensuring consistent VLAN configurations and trunk settings, administrators can prevent VLAN-related connectivity issues and maintain network connectivity.

Moreover, link aggregation problems, such as misconfigured EtherChannel bundles or inconsistent channel configurations, can lead to packet loss and suboptimal load balancing. Administrators can troubleshoot EtherChannel issues using the "show etherchannel summary" command to verify

EtherChannel status and member interfaces. Additionally, verifying consistency in EtherChannel configurations, such as port-channel modes, load-balancing methods, and member interface settings, can help resolve link aggregation problems and ensure optimal performance.

In summary, Layer 2 troubleshooting is essential for maintaining the integrity and reliability of network connectivity. By identifying and resolving data link layer problems promptly, administrators can minimize downtime and ensure seamless communication between network devices. Through the use of diagnostic commands, such as "show interfaces," "show spanning-tree," and "show mac address-table," administrators can effectively diagnose and address Layer 2 issues, optimizing network performance and enhancing overall network reliability.

Chapter 4: Addressing Common Layer 3 Routing Problems

Layer 3 troubleshooting involves addressing routing protocol issues, which are critical for ensuring efficient packet forwarding and connectivity between devices across different network segments. One common routing protocol issue is route flapping, where routes repeatedly alternate between active and inactive states, causing instability and suboptimal routing decisions. Administrators can diagnose route flapping using routing protocol debug commands to monitor route advertisements and withdrawals, identifying the source of route instability and implementing route dampening to suppress flapping routes and stabilize the routing table.

Another prevalent problem is route summarization errors, where incorrect summarization configurations result in suboptimal routing and inefficient use of network resources. Administrators can use the "show ip route" command to examine the routing table and identify summarization boundaries, ensuring summary routes cover all necessary subnets without over-summarizing or creating routing black holes. Additionally, validating summarization configurations and adjusting summarization boundaries as needed can optimize routing efficiency and reduce routing overhead.

Moreover, routing protocol convergence issues can occur due to network topology changes or link failures, resulting in delayed convergence and prolonged network downtime. Administrators can troubleshoot convergence problems using routing protocol monitoring commands to track routing updates and convergence times, identifying bottlenecks or configuration errors that impede convergence. By optimizing routing protocol timers, tuning convergence parameters, and implementing fast convergence mechanisms like BFD (Bidirectional Forwarding Detection), administrators can expedite convergence and minimize network downtime.

Additionally, misconfigured route redistribution can lead to routing loops, black-holing, or routing inconsistencies between different routing domains. Administrators can troubleshoot redistribution issues by examining redistribution configurations and route redistribution tables to ensure consistent route propagation and filtering. Validating route redistribution filters, route maps, and redistribution metrics can help prevent unintended route redistribution and maintain routing stability across heterogeneous networks.

Furthermore, incorrect routing protocol authentication settings can compromise network security and integrity, allowing unauthorized devices to inject false routing information or disrupt routing operations. Administrators can verify authentication configurations using routing protocol authentication commands to ensure that neighboring routers authenticate routing updates using the correct authentication keys or passwords. Additionally, enabling message digest authentication (MD5) or implementing IPsec VPN tunnels between routing peers can enhance routing protocol security and protect against malicious routing attacks.

Moreover, troubleshooting routing protocol neighbor adjacencies involves verifying neighbor configurations, interface settings, and network connectivity to ensure that routing peers can establish and maintain neighbor relationships successfully. Administrators can use the "show ip ospf neighbor" or "show ip bgp summary" command to display neighbor status and adjacency information, identifying failed or flapping neighbors and diagnosing underlying connectivity issues. By resolving neighbor adjacency problems promptly, administrators can restore routing protocol stability and maintain network connectivity.

In summary, Layer 3 troubleshooting is essential for identifying and resolving routing protocol issues that impact network performance and reliability. By leveraging diagnostic commands, protocol monitoring tools, and best practices, administrators can effectively troubleshoot routing protocol problems, optimize routing operations, and ensure seamless communication between network devices. Through proactive monitoring, configuration validation, and timely intervention, administrators can minimize downtime, improve network resilience, and enhance overall network efficiency.

Routing table analysis and troubleshooting techniques are crucial for network administrators to maintain optimal network performance and troubleshoot connectivity issues effectively. The routing table serves as a critical component of the network infrastructure, containing information about available routes and next-hop destinations for packet forwarding. By analyzing the routing table, administrators can diagnose routing problems, optimize routing decisions, and ensure efficient packet delivery across the network.

One common troubleshooting technique involves examining the routing table to identify route inconsistencies, missing routes, or incorrect route entries. Administrators can use the "show ip route" command on Cisco routers to display the routing table and inspect route entries, including network prefixes, next-hop addresses, administrative distances, and route types. By scrutinizing the routing table output, administrators can detect anomalies such as unreachable destinations, route flapping, or routing loops that may impact network connectivity.

Moreover, analyzing the routing table's contents can help administrators assess routing protocol behavior, convergence status, and routing protocol preferences. By comparing route entries learned from different routing protocols or sources, administrators can evaluate route selection criteria, route redistribution policies, and routing protocol metrics. For instance, administrators can use the "show ip route ospf" or "show ip route bgp" commands to view OSPF or BGP route entries specifically, allowing them to identify protocol-specific routing issues and troubleshoot protocol-specific problems accordingly.

Additionally, route summarization analysis is essential for optimizing routing table size, reducing routing overhead, and improving network scalability. Administrators can review summarized route entries in the routing table to verify proper summarization boundaries, ensuring that summarized routes cover relevant subnets without over-summarizing or creating routing black holes. By examining summary routes and their associated subnets, administrators can validate summarization configurations, adjust summarization boundaries as needed, and optimize routing efficiency.

Furthermore, troubleshooting routing loops involves identifying and mitigating routing loops that can occur due to misconfigured routing protocols, incorrect static routes, or network topology changes. Administrators can use the "traceroute" command to trace the path of packets through the network and identify potential routing loops or routing loops. By analyzing traceroute output and inspecting routing table entries along the packet's path, administrators can pinpoint the source of routing loops and implement corrective measures such as route filtering, route dampening, or route summarization to prevent loop formation and restore routing stability.

Moreover, route preference analysis allows administrators to understand how routers select best paths and make routing decisions based on routing protocol metrics, administrative distances, and route types. By examining route attributes such as metric values, route tags, or route attributes, administrators can evaluate route preferences and troubleshoot routing inconsistencies or suboptimal routing decisions. For example, administrators can compare route metrics between OSPF and BGP routes to identify discrepancies and adjust routing protocol metrics or route preferences to influence route selection.

Additionally, analyzing route redistribution configurations and troubleshooting route redistribution issues is essential for maintaining routing integrity and ensuring seamless communication between different routing domains or protocols. Administrators can verify route redistribution configurations, examine redistribution filters, and monitor route redistribution tables to ensure consistent route propagation and prevent routing inconsistencies. By validating redistribution policies, resolving redistribution conflicts, and verifying route redistribution filters, administrators can troubleshoot route redistribution problems and maintain routing stability.

In summary, routing table analysis and troubleshooting techniques are indispensable for network administrators to diagnose routing problems, optimize routing decisions, and ensure reliable network connectivity. By leveraging diagnostic commands, protocol monitoring tools, and best practices, administrators can effectively analyze routing tables, troubleshoot routing issues, and maintain network resilience. Through proactive monitoring, configuration validation, and timely intervention, administrators can minimize downtime, improve routing efficiency, and enhance overall network performance.

Chapter 5: Troubleshooting WAN (Wide Area Network) Connectivity

WAN troubleshooting is an essential aspect of network management, focusing on diagnosing and resolving connectivity issues that affect Wide Area Network (WAN) links and services. In today's interconnected world, WANs play a crucial role in enabling communication between geographically dispersed locations, supporting critical business applications, and facilitating data exchange across distributed environments. However, WANs are susceptible to various problems such as link failures, latency issues, bandwidth constraints, and configuration errors, necessitating robust troubleshooting strategies to ensure uninterrupted connectivity and optimal performance.

One of the fundamental aspects of WAN troubleshooting is identifying the root cause of connectivity problems, which often requires a systematic approach and the use of diagnostic tools. Administrators can begin by conducting preliminary assessments to gather information about the affected WAN links, including link status, interface configurations, and traffic utilization. Command-line interface (CLI) commands such as "show interface" and "show ip route" can provide valuable insights into interface status, bandwidth utilization, and routing information, helping administrators pinpoint potential issues and determine the scope of troubleshooting efforts.

Furthermore, WAN troubleshooting involves verifying WAN link configurations and addressing common configuration errors that can impede connectivity or degrade performance. Administrators should ensure that WAN interfaces are properly configured with correct IP addressing, subnet masks, encapsulation types, and interface settings such as duplex and speed parameters. By reviewing interface configurations and comparing them against established standards or best practices, administrators can identify misconfigurations, inconsistencies, or compatibility issues that may impact WAN connectivity.

Moreover, WAN troubleshooting often entails diagnosing link-related problems such as link flapping, packet loss, or jitter that can degrade application performance and user experience. Administrators can leverage network monitoring tools such as SNMP-based monitoring systems or packet capture tools like Wireshark to analyze WAN link behavior, monitor link utilization, and identify anomalies in network traffic patterns. By examining performance metrics such as latency, jitter, and packet loss, administrators can assess link quality, detect performance bottlenecks, and troubleshoot issues affecting WAN connectivity.

In addition to link-related issues, WAN troubleshooting also involves addressing routing problems that can disrupt traffic flow and impair communication between network endpoints. Routing issues may arise due to misconfigured routing protocols, route summarization errors, or routing table inconsistencies that result in suboptimal path selection or packet drops. Administrators can use CLI commands like "show ip bgp" or "show ip ospf neighbor" to examine routing protocol status, neighbor relationships, and route advertisements, facilitating the identification of routing problems and the implementation of corrective actions.

Furthermore, WAN troubleshooting encompasses troubleshooting WAN optimization solutions deployed to enhance network performance, mitigate bandwidth constraints, and improve application delivery across WAN links. WAN optimization technologies such as data compression, deduplication, and traffic prioritization can introduce complexities and interoperability issues that require careful configuration and monitoring. Administrators should verify the proper functioning of WAN optimization devices, validate optimization policies, and analyze performance metrics to ensure that optimization techniques effectively meet the organization's requirements without compromising network stability or introducing latency.

Moreover, WAN troubleshooting extends to addressing connectivity issues related to WAN service providers, third-party network connections, or interconnection points such as Internet gateways or MPLS (Multiprotocol Label Switching) peering links. When troubleshooting external connectivity problems, administrators may need to collaborate with service providers, perform traceroute tests, or analyze network traffic to identify points of failure or performance degradation. By engaging with service provider support teams and conducting thorough diagnostics, administrators can expedite issue resolution and minimize service disruptions affecting WAN connectivity.

Additionally, WAN troubleshooting encompasses disaster recovery planning and failover testing to ensure business continuity in the event of WAN link failures or network outages. Administrators should implement redundant WAN links, configure failover mechanisms, and test failover procedures regularly to verify the effectiveness of redundancy configurations and validate the organization's ability to maintain connectivity during adverse conditions. By simulating failure scenarios, conducting failover tests, and documenting recovery procedures, administrators can enhance network resilience and mitigate the impact of WAN-related disruptions on critical business operations.

In summary, WAN troubleshooting is a critical competency for network administrators tasked with maintaining WAN connectivity, optimizing network performance, and ensuring seamless communication across distributed environments. By adopting a systematic approach, leveraging diagnostic tools, and collaborating with stakeholders, administrators can diagnose and resolve WAN-related issues efficiently, minimize downtime, and uphold service levels to meet organizational objectives. Through proactive monitoring, configuration management, and continuous improvement initiatives, administrators can enhance WAN reliability, resilience, and responsiveness to support evolving business requirements and technological advancements in today's dynamic networking landscape.

Troubleshooting WAN link issues and performance problems is a crucial aspect of network management, ensuring optimal connectivity and efficient data transmission across geographically dispersed locations. WAN links serve as the backbone of modern enterprise networks, facilitating communication between remote sites, supporting mission-critical applications, and enabling access to centralized resources. However, WAN link issues such as connectivity disruptions, bandwidth constraints, and latency issues can adversely affect application performance, user experience, and overall productivity, underscoring the importance of timely diagnosis and resolution.

One common challenge in troubleshooting WAN link issues is identifying the root cause of connectivity problems, which often requires a methodical approach and the use of diagnostic tools to gather relevant information and assess link performance. Administrators can leverage command-line interface (CLI) commands such as "show interface," "ping," and "traceroute" to examine interface status, test connectivity to remote destinations, and trace the path of network packets across the WAN. By analyzing interface statistics, checking for errors or anomalies, and verifying end-to-end reachability, administrators can gain insights into the health and behavior of WAN links.

Moreover, WAN link troubleshooting entails verifying WAN link configurations and addressing configuration errors that may impact link connectivity or performance. Administrators should ensure that WAN interfaces are correctly configured with appropriate IP addressing, subnet masks, encapsulation types, and interface settings such as speed and duplex settings. Additionally, administrators should validate routing configurations, including static routes, dynamic routing protocols, and Quality of Service (QoS) policies, to ensure that traffic is appropriately routed and prioritized across WAN links.

Furthermore, WAN link issues often manifest as performance problems related to bandwidth utilization, congestion, or packet loss, affecting the responsiveness and reliability of network services. Administrators can employ network monitoring tools such as SNMP-based monitoring systems, NetFlow analyzers, or packet capture tools to assess WAN link performance, monitor traffic patterns, and identify bottlenecks or anomalies in network traffic. By analyzing performance metrics such as throughput, latency, and error rates, administrators can pinpoint areas of contention, troubleshoot performance issues, and implement optimization measures to improve WAN link efficiency.

In addition to performance monitoring, WAN link troubleshooting involves diagnosing link-related problems such as link flapping, interface errors, or physical layer issues that can disrupt connectivity and degrade link stability. Administrators should inspect physical cabling, connectors, and interface hardware for signs of damage, corrosion, or improper termination that may affect signal integrity or transmission quality. Additionally, administrators can use loopback tests, cable testers, or optical time-domain reflectometers (OTDRs) to verify cable continuity, detect faults, and localize physical layer issues affecting WAN link connectivity.

Moreover, WAN link troubleshooting encompasses troubleshooting WAN optimization solutions deployed to enhance network performance, mitigate bandwidth constraints, and improve application delivery across WAN links. WAN optimization technologies such as data compression, deduplication, and caching can introduce complexities and interoperability issues that require careful configuration and monitoring. Administrators should verify the proper functioning of WAN optimization devices, validate optimization policies, and analyze performance metrics to ensure that optimization techniques effectively meet the organization's requirements without compromising network stability or introducing latency.

Additionally, WAN link troubleshooting extends to addressing connectivity issues related to WAN service providers, third-party network connections, or interconnection points such as Internet gateways or MPLS (Multiprotocol Label Switching) peering links. When troubleshooting external connectivity problems, administrators may need to collaborate with service providers, perform traceroute tests, or analyze network traffic to identify points of failure or performance degradation. By engaging with service provider support teams and conducting thorough diagnostics, administrators can expedite issue resolution and minimize service disruptions affecting WAN connectivity.

Furthermore, WAN link troubleshooting encompasses disaster recovery planning and failover testing to ensure business continuity in the event of WAN link failures or network outages. Administrators should implement redundant WAN links, configure failover mechanisms, and test failover procedures regularly to verify the effectiveness of redundancy configurations and validate the organization's ability to maintain connectivity during adverse conditions. By simulating failure scenarios, conducting failover tests, and documenting recovery procedures, administrators can enhance network resilience and mitigate the impact of WAN-related disruptions on critical business operations.

In summary, troubleshooting WAN link issues and performance problems requires a comprehensive understanding of WAN technologies, meticulous attention to detail, and proficiency in using diagnostic tools and CLI commands to identify and resolve connectivity issues. By adopting a systematic approach, leveraging diagnostic techniques, and collaborating with stakeholders, administrators can diagnose and remediate WAN link problems efficiently, minimize downtime, and optimize WAN performance to support organizational objectives and meet user expectations in today's interconnected business environment.

Chapter 6: Dealing with Network Security Incidents and Threats

Network security incident response procedures are essential protocols implemented by organizations to detect, assess, and mitigate security breaches, unauthorized access, or malicious activities targeting their network infrastructure and assets. These procedures aim to minimize the impact of security incidents, preserve the integrity of sensitive information, and restore normal operations swiftly to safeguard business continuity and mitigate financial and reputational risks associated with cybersecurity incidents.

The incident response process typically begins with the detection of anomalous behavior, suspicious network activity, or security alerts generated by intrusion detection systems (IDS), intrusion prevention systems (IPS), security information and event management (SIEM) platforms, or other monitoring tools. Upon detection, network administrators initiate incident response procedures to investigate the nature and scope of the security incident, classify its severity, and determine the appropriate response actions.

One of the first steps in network security incident response is to gather relevant information and evidence related to the incident, which may involve capturing network traffic, log files, system snapshots, or other forensic data to facilitate root cause analysis and attribution of the security breach. Command-line interface (CLI) commands such as "tcpdump," "netstat," and "grep" can be used to capture and analyze network packets, monitor network connections, and search log files for indicators of compromise (IOCs) or suspicious activities.

Subsequently, incident responders conduct a comprehensive analysis of the incident, examining the attack vectors, methods used by threat actors, and potential impact on the organization's network infrastructure, systems, and data. This analysis may involve correlating security events, conducting vulnerability assessments, and reviewing access logs to identify the entry points and lateral movement of attackers within the network.

Based on the severity and impact of the security incident, incident responders prioritize response actions and containment measures to mitigate the immediate risks and prevent further unauthorized access or data exfiltration. CLI commands such as "iptables" or "firewall-cmd" can be used to implement access control lists (ACLs), block malicious IP addresses, or restrict network traffic to contain the spread of malware or unauthorized activities.

Simultaneously, incident responders collaborate with internal stakeholders, such as IT security teams, network operations personnel, and business units, as well as external parties, including law enforcement agencies, regulatory authorities, and third-party vendors, to coordinate response efforts, share threat intelligence, and address legal and compliance requirements associated with security incidents.

Furthermore, incident response procedures encompass communication and notification protocols to keep relevant stakeholders informed about the security incident, its impact, and the remediation measures being undertaken. This may involve drafting incident reports, communicating with executive management, preparing public statements, and notifying affected parties, such as customers, partners, or regulatory bodies, in compliance with data breach notification laws and regulations.

In addition to containment and communication, incident response procedures include the eradication of malicious artifacts, vulnerabilities, or compromised assets from the network environment to restore the integrity and security of affected systems. This may entail removing malware infections, patching software vulnerabilities, resetting compromised user accounts or credentials, and restoring data from backups to recover from data loss or corruption resulting from the security incident.

Moreover, incident responders conduct post-incident analysis and lessons learned sessions to evaluate the effectiveness of incident response procedures, identify gaps or shortcomings in security controls, and implement corrective actions to strengthen the organization's security posture and resilience against future security incidents. This continuous improvement process may involve updating security policies, enhancing threat detection capabilities, providing additional training to staff, and refining incident response playbooks based on insights gained from real-world incidents.

In summary, network security incident response procedures are critical components of an organization's cybersecurity strategy, enabling timely detection, containment, and remediation of security incidents to mitigate their impact on business operations and safeguard sensitive information assets. By adopting a systematic and proactive approach to incident response, organizations can effectively mitigate cyber threats, minimize downtime, and protect their reputation and brand integrity in today's evolving threat landscape.

Identifying and mitigating network security threats is a fundamental aspect of maintaining the integrity, confidentiality, and availability of an organization's information technology infrastructure. In today's interconnected digital landscape, where cyber threats continue to evolve and proliferate, organizations must remain vigilant and proactive in detecting and neutralizing potential security risks to safeguard their critical assets and data.

One of the primary challenges in identifying network security threats is the diverse range of attack vectors and tactics employed by cyber adversaries to exploit vulnerabilities and infiltrate networks. These threats may include malware infections, phishing attacks, distributed denial-of-service (DDoS) attacks, insider threats, and advanced persistent threats (APTs), among others. To effectively counter these threats, organizations must adopt a multi-layered approach to security that encompasses preventive, detective, and responsive measures.

Preventive measures aim to reduce the attack surface and fortify the organization's defenses against potential threats. This involves implementing robust security controls, such as firewalls, intrusion prevention systems (IPS), antivirus software, and email filtering solutions, to block malicious traffic, prevent unauthorized access, and thwart phishing attempts. Additionally, organizations should regularly patch and update software and firmware to address known vulnerabilities and minimize the risk of exploitation by cyber attackers.

Command: Updating software and firmware can be accomplished using specific commands depending on the operating system and platform. For example, in a Linux environment, the "apt-get update" command is commonly used to update package repositories and the "apt-get upgrade" command to install available updates. Similarly, in a Cisco networking environment, the "show version" command can be used to check the current firmware version, and the "copy" command to install new firmware images.

Detective measures involve continuous monitoring and analysis of network traffic, system logs, and security events to identify anomalous behavior, potential security incidents, or indicators of compromise (IOCs). This includes deploying intrusion detection systems (IDS), security information and event management (SIEM) solutions, and endpoint detection and response

(EDR) tools to detect and alert on suspicious activities, unauthorized access attempts, or malware infections.

Command: Tools such as "tcpdump" and "Wireshark" can be used to capture and analyze network packets, while the "tail" command can be employed to monitor log files in real-time for any unusual activity. In addition, SIEM platforms often provide command-line interfaces or APIs for querying and analyzing security event data collected from various sources.

Once a security threat has been identified, organizations must respond promptly to mitigate its impact and prevent further damage. This may involve isolating compromised systems, blocking malicious IP addresses, disabling compromised user accounts, or quarantining infected devices to contain the spread of malware or unauthorized access. Incident response playbooks and predefined response procedures can help streamline the response process and ensure consistency in the actions taken.

Command: Depending on the nature of the security incident, various CLI commands can be used to implement containment measures. For example, in a Linux environment, the "iptables" command can be used to configure firewall rules to block traffic from specific IP addresses or ports. Similarly, in a Windows environment, the "netsh advfirewall" command can be used to manage Windows Firewall settings.

In addition to preventive and detective measures, organizations must also focus on building resilience and preparedness to effectively respond to and recover from security incidents. This includes conducting regular security awareness training for employees, developing incident response plans, and performing tabletop exercises and simulations to test the organization's readiness to handle various security scenarios.

Command: Training and readiness activities can be facilitated through the use of simulated attack scenarios and interactive training modules. For example, organizations can use penetration testing tools such as "Metasploit" or "Nmap" to simulate cyber attacks and assess the effectiveness of their defenses. Additionally, security awareness training platforms often provide interactive modules and quizzes to educate employees about common security threats and best practices.

Furthermore, organizations should engage in threat intelligence sharing and collaboration with industry peers, government agencies, and cybersecurity communities to stay abreast of emerging threats, vulnerabilities, and attack trends. By sharing information about security incidents, threat actors, and defensive strategies, organizations can enhance their collective resilience and strengthen their defenses against evolving cyber threats.

Command: Threat intelligence sharing platforms and information sharing and analysis centers (ISACs) often provide APIs or data feeds that can be integrated with security tools and platforms to enrich threat detection and response capabilities. Additionally, organizations can use command-line tools such as "curl" or "wget" to retrieve threat intelligence feeds from external sources and ingest them into their security systems for analysis.

In summary, identifying and mitigating network security threats require a comprehensive and proactive approach that combines preventive, detective, and responsive measures. By leveraging technology, best practices, and collaboration, organizations can effectively defend against cyber threats and protect their critical assets and data from unauthorized access, manipulation, or theft. Continual monitoring, assessment, and adaptation are essential to staying ahead of evolving cyber threats and maintaining a resilient security posture in today's dynamic threat landscape.

Chapter 7: Performance Tuning and Optimization Techniques

Network performance monitoring is crucial for maintaining the health, efficiency, and reliability of an organization's network infrastructure. In today's interconnected and data-driven business environment, where networks serve as the backbone of communication and data exchange, monitoring tools and techniques play a vital role in ensuring optimal network performance and identifying potential issues before they escalate into significant disruptions.

One of the fundamental aspects of network performance monitoring is the collection and analysis of key performance indicators (KPIs) that provide insights into the overall health and performance of the network. These KPIs include metrics such as bandwidth utilization, latency, packet loss, jitter, throughput, and error rates, which are essential for assessing network performance and diagnosing potential bottlenecks or issues.

Command: Various command-line tools can be used to collect network performance metrics. For example, the "ping" command can be used to measure round-trip time (RTT) and packet loss to a specific destination, while the "traceroute" command can be used to identify the network path taken by packets and measure hop-by-hop latency. Additionally, tools like "iperf" or "iperf3" can be used to measure network throughput between two endpoints.

Network performance monitoring tools come in various forms, ranging from simple command-line utilities to sophisticated network management systems (NMS) with comprehensive monitoring and reporting capabilities. These tools use various techniques such as SNMP (Simple Network Management Protocol) polling, packet sniffing, flow analysis, and synthetic transactions to gather data about network performance and behavior.

Command: SNMP is a widely used protocol for monitoring and managing network devices. Tools like "snmpwalk" or "snmpget" can be used to query SNMP-enabled devices for performance data, such as interface statistics, CPU utilization, memory usage, and error counters. Additionally, packet sniffing tools like "tcpdump" or "Wireshark" can capture and analyze network traffic to identify performance issues or anomalies.

Flow analysis tools, such as NetFlow, sFlow, or IPFIX, provide visibility into traffic patterns and behavior by collecting and analyzing flow records exported by routers, switches, and other network devices. These flow records contain information about the source and destination IP addresses, ports, protocols, and amount of data transferred, allowing administrators to identify top talkers, understand application usage, and detect anomalies or security threats.

Command: Configuring flow export on network devices involves enabling the appropriate flow protocol (e.g.,

NetFlow, sFlow) and specifying the destination collector IP address and port. For example, on Cisco routers and switches, commands like "ip flow-export" or "sflow collector" can be used to configure flow export parameters.

Synthetic transaction monitoring involves simulating user transactions or interactions with networked applications and services to measure response times, availability, and performance. This approach helps identify performance issues from the end user's perspective and ensure that critical applications and services meet service level agreements (SLAs) and performance targets.

Command: Tools like "curl" or "wget" can be used to perform synthetic transactions by sending HTTP requests to web servers and measuring response times. Similarly, utilities like "ping" or "telnet" can be used to test network connectivity and measure round-trip times to specific destinations.

In addition to monitoring network performance in real-time, historical performance data and trends are essential for capacity planning, trend analysis, and forecasting future network requirements. Network performance monitoring tools often include reporting and analytics features that allow administrators to generate custom reports, dashboards, and graphs to visualize performance metrics over time and identify long-term trends or recurring issues.

Command: Many network monitoring tools provide command-line interfaces or APIs for retrieving historical performance data and generating reports. For example, commands like "curl" or "wget" can be used to retrieve data from RESTful APIs exposed by monitoring tools, while scripting languages like Python or PowerShell can be used to automate report generation and analysis tasks.

In summary, network performance monitoring tools and techniques are essential for maintaining the health, efficiency, and reliability of modern network infrastructures. By collecting, analyzing, and interpreting performance data, organizations can identify potential issues, optimize network resources, and ensure the smooth operation of critical business processes. Continual monitoring, analysis, and adaptation are key to maximizing network performance and delivering a seamless user experience in today's dynamic and interconnected digital environments.

Performance optimization is a critical aspect of network management, aimed at ensuring that networks operate efficiently and meet the demands of modern digital environments. In today's interconnected world, where businesses rely heavily on network infrastructure for communication, collaboration, and data exchange, optimizing network performance is essential for delivering a seamless user experience, maximizing productivity, and maintaining competitive advantage.

One of the key strategies for optimizing network performance is to design and configure the network infrastructure with scalability, reliability, and performance in mind. This involves carefully planning the network topology, selecting the appropriate hardware and software components, and implementing best practices for network design and configuration.

Command: CLI commands such as "show running-config" on Cisco devices or "display current-configuration" on Huawei devices can be used to view the current configuration of network devices, including interfaces, routing protocols, and quality of service (QoS) settings.

Proper network segmentation and traffic isolation are essential for optimizing performance, as they help reduce congestion, minimize broadcast domains, and improve overall network efficiency. VLANs (Virtual Local Area Networks) can be used to segment network traffic logically, while access control lists (ACLs) can be employed to control traffic flow and enforce security policies between different network segments.

Command: Commands like "vlan" on Cisco switches or "vlan batch" on Huawei switches can be used to create VLANs, while "access-list" commands can be used to define ACLs and filter traffic based on specific criteria such as source or destination IP addresses, ports, or protocols.

Quality of service (QoS) mechanisms can be deployed to prioritize network traffic and ensure that critical applications and services receive the necessary bandwidth and latency requirements. QoS techniques such as traffic shaping, traffic policing, and priority queuing can be used to control and prioritize traffic based on predefined policies and service level agreements (SLAs).

Command: Commands like "policy-map" and "class-map" on Cisco devices or "traffic policy" on Huawei devices can be used to define QoS policies, while commands like "shaping" or "policer" can be used to configure traffic shaping or policing parameters.

Optimizing network performance also involves monitoring and managing network resources effectively. This includes tracking key performance indicators (KPIs), such as bandwidth utilization, latency, packet loss, and throughput, and proactively addressing any performance issues or bottlenecks that may arise.

Command: Network monitoring tools like "snmpwalk" or "snmpget" can be used to query SNMP-enabled devices for performance data, while commands like "show interface" can be used to display interface statistics and utilization.

Regular network performance testing and benchmarking are essential for identifying potential performance bottlenecks and evaluating the effectiveness of performance optimization strategies. By conducting periodic performance tests and measurements, network administrators can identify areas for improvement and implement corrective actions to enhance network performance and reliability.

Command: Tools like "iperf" or "ping" can be used to perform network performance tests, measure throughput, latency, and packet loss, and identify potential issues affecting network performance.

Another important aspect of performance optimization is ensuring that network devices are properly configured and maintained to operate at optimal performance levels. This includes keeping device firmware and software up to date, implementing security best practices, and optimizing device settings for performance and reliability.

Command: Commands like "upgrade" or "install" can be used to upgrade device firmware or software, while commands like "crypto key generate rsa" can be used to generate cryptographic keys for secure communication.

In summary, performance optimization is a continuous process that requires careful planning, implementation, and monitoring to ensure that network infrastructure operates at peak efficiency and meets the demands of modern digital environments. By following best practices, deploying appropriate technologies, and proactively addressing performance issues, organizations can maximize the performance, reliability, and scalability of their networks, ultimately enabling them to achieve their business objectives more effectively.

Chapter 8: Advanced Troubleshooting with Network Monitoring Tools

Network monitoring tools are essential components of modern IT infrastructure, providing visibility into network performance, availability, and security posture. The selection and configuration of these tools play a crucial role in ensuring effective monitoring and management of network resources. With a plethora of options available in the market, choosing the right network monitoring tool can be challenging. However, by understanding the requirements of the network environment and evaluating key features and capabilities, organizations can make informed decisions to select the most suitable tool for their needs.

One of the first steps in selecting a network monitoring tool is to define the specific monitoring requirements and objectives of the organization. This involves identifying the types of devices and technologies that need to be monitored, such as routers, switches, firewalls, servers, and applications, as well as the key performance metrics and KPIs that need to be tracked. Additionally, consideration should be given to scalability, ease of deployment, integration capabilities, and cost-effectiveness.

Command: Commands like "show version" on Cisco devices or "display version" on Huawei devices can be used to view device information, including hardware and software versions.

Once the monitoring requirements are established, organizations can begin evaluating different network monitoring tools based on their features, functionalities, and compatibility with existing infrastructure. Some of the key features to look for in a network monitoring tool include real-time monitoring, historical data analysis, alerting and notification capabilities, customizable dashboards and reports, support for multiple vendors and technologies, and scalability for large-scale deployments.

Command: Commands like "show interface" or "show ip route" on Cisco devices or "display interface" or "display ip routing-table" on Huawei devices can be used to view interface statistics and routing information.

Popular network monitoring tools such as SolarWinds Network Performance Monitor (NPM), PRTG Network Monitor, Nagios Core, Zabbix, and Cisco Prime Infrastructure offer a wide range of features and capabilities to meet diverse monitoring needs. These tools provide comprehensive visibility into network performance metrics such as bandwidth utilization, latency, packet loss, device health, and application performance, allowing organizations to proactively identify and address issues before they impact end users.

Command: Commands like "ping" or "traceroute" can be used to test network connectivity and diagnose connectivity issues, while commands like "show tech-support" can be used to generate detailed diagnostic information for troubleshooting purposes.

Once a network monitoring tool is selected, the next step is to configure it according to the specific requirements of the organization. This involves setting up device discovery, configuring monitoring parameters and thresholds, defining alerting and notification rules, and customizing dashboards and reports to visualize performance data effectively. Additionally, integration with other IT management systems such as ticketing systems, configuration management databases (CMDBs), and IT service management (ITSM) platforms can enhance the overall effectiveness of network monitoring and management.

Command: Configuration commands such as "snmp-server community" on Cisco devices or "snmp-agent community" on Huawei devices can be used to configure SNMP community strings for device monitoring.

Regular maintenance and updates are essential to ensure the continued effectiveness of network monitoring tools. This includes keeping the tool software up to date with the latest patches and updates, configuring regular backups of monitoring configurations and data, and performing periodic audits to validate the accuracy and reliability of monitoring data. Additionally, ongoing training and skill development for network administrators and operators are crucial to maximizing the value and utility of network monitoring tools.

Command: Commands like "show version" on Cisco devices or "display version" on Huawei devices can be used to check the software version of network monitoring tools, while commands like "backup" or "export" can be used to create backups of monitoring configurations and data.

In summary, the selection and configuration of network monitoring tools are critical tasks that require careful consideration and planning. By understanding the specific monitoring requirements of the organization, evaluating key features and capabilities of different tools, and configuring the selected tool according to best practices and industry standards, organizations can effectively monitor and manage their network infrastructure, ensure optimal performance and availability, and mitigate security risks and vulnerabilities.

Advanced troubleshooting using monitoring data involves leveraging the wealth of information collected by network monitoring tools to diagnose and resolve complex issues within a network environment. This approach goes beyond basic fault detection and resolution, enabling network administrators to gain deeper insights into network behavior, identify root causes of problems, and implement targeted remediation strategies. By analyzing historical performance data, correlating events, and applying advanced troubleshooting techniques, organizations can improve network reliability, optimize performance, and enhance overall operational efficiency.

Command: Commands like "show interface" or "show ip route" on Cisco devices or "display interface" or "display ip routing-table" on Huawei devices can be used to view interface statistics and routing information.

One of the key components of advanced troubleshooting using monitoring data is the ability to collect and analyze comprehensive data from across the network infrastructure. This includes monitoring network traffic, device performance metrics, application behavior, and security events in real-time, as well as capturing historical data for trend analysis and capacity planning. Network monitoring tools such as SolarWinds Network Performance Monitor (NPM), PRTG Network Monitor, and Nagios Core offer powerful features for data collection, analysis, and visualization, enabling administrators to gain actionable insights into network performance and behavior.

Command: Configuration commands such as "snmp-server community" on Cisco devices or "snmp-agent community" on Huawei devices can be used to configure SNMP community strings for device monitoring.

Advanced troubleshooting often involves correlating different types of monitoring data to identify patterns, trends, and anomalies that may indicate underlying issues or potential performance bottlenecks. For example, correlating network traffic data with device performance metrics can help pinpoint bandwidth-intensive applications or devices causing congestion on the network. Similarly, correlating security event logs with network traffic data can help detect and mitigate security threats such as DDoS attacks or malware infections.

Command: Commands like "ping" or "traceroute" can be used to test network connectivity and diagnose connectivity issues, while commands like "show tech-support" can be used to generate detailed diagnostic information for troubleshooting purposes.

In addition to correlating data from different sources, advanced troubleshooting techniques may also involve the use of packet capture and analysis tools to inspect individual packets traversing the network. Packet capture tools such as Wireshark or tcpdump allow administrators to capture, analyze, and decode network traffic in real-time, enabling them to identify protocol errors, packet drops, latency issues, and other network anomalies. By examining packet headers and payloads, administrators can gain deeper insights into the behavior of network protocols and applications, facilitating more targeted troubleshooting and problem resolution.

Command: Packet capture commands such as "monitor capture" on Cisco devices or "capture packet" on Huawei devices can be used to capture network traffic for analysis.

Furthermore, advanced troubleshooting using monitoring data often involves the use of diagnostic commands and utilities available on network devices themselves. These commands provide detailed information about device configuration, status, and performance, allowing administrators to perform in-depth analysis and troubleshooting directly on the affected devices. For example, commands such as "show running-config" and "show interface" on Cisco devices or "display current-configuration" and "display interface" on Huawei devices provide valuable insights into device configuration and interface status, which can help identify misconfigurations, hardware failures, or other issues affecting network performance.

Command: Diagnostic commands such as "show tech-support" on Cisco devices or "display diagnostic-information" on Huawei devices can be used to generate detailed diagnostic information for troubleshooting purposes.

In summary, advanced troubleshooting using monitoring data is a powerful approach for diagnosing and resolving complex network issues. By collecting and analyzing comprehensive data from across the network infrastructure, correlating different types of monitoring data, leveraging packet capture and analysis tools, and using diagnostic commands available on network devices, administrators can gain deeper insights into network behavior, identify root causes of problems, and implement targeted remediation strategies to optimize network performance and reliability.

Chapter 9: Resolving VoIP (Voice over IP) and Video Conferencing Issues

Troubleshooting VoIP call quality issues is an essential aspect of maintaining a reliable and high-performing voice communication system. In today's digital age, Voice over Internet Protocol (VoIP) has become the preferred choice for businesses and organizations worldwide, offering cost-effective and feature-rich telephony services over IP networks. However, ensuring optimal call quality can be challenging due to various factors such as network congestion, packet loss, latency, jitter, and hardware or software issues. To effectively troubleshoot VoIP call quality problems, network administrators must employ a systematic approach that involves identifying, isolating, and resolving the underlying causes of poor call quality.

One common VoIP call quality issue is packet loss, which occurs when packets of voice data are dropped or discarded during transmission over the network. Packet loss can result in choppy or distorted audio, delays, and dropped calls, severely impacting the user experience. To diagnose packet loss issues, network administrators can use network monitoring tools to analyze network traffic and identify areas of congestion or packet drops. Additionally, packet capture and analysis tools such as Wireshark can be used to inspect packet headers and payloads, allowing administrators to pinpoint the source of packet loss and take corrective action.

Another factor that can affect VoIP call quality is latency, which refers to the delay experienced by voice packets as they travel between endpoints. High latency can lead to delays in audio transmission, causing issues such as echo, voice overlap, and out-of-sync conversations. To troubleshoot latency issues, administrators can use network diagnostic tools to measure round-trip times (RTT) between endpoints and identify areas of excessive delay. By optimizing network routing, reducing network congestion, and prioritizing VoIP traffic through Quality of Service (QoS) policies, administrators can minimize latency and improve call quality.

Jitter is another common issue that can degrade VoIP call quality, particularly over congested or unreliable network connections. Jitter refers to the variation in packet arrival times, resulting in uneven audio playback and jittery voice quality. To mitigate jitter, administrators can implement jitter buffer mechanisms on VoIP endpoints or routers to smooth out variations in packet arrival times. Additionally, deploying jitter buffering algorithms and adjusting buffer sizes can help compensate for network jitter and ensure consistent audio quality during VoIP calls.

Command: Commands like "ping" or "traceroute" can be used to test network connectivity and measure round-trip times between endpoints, while commands like "show interface" can be used to monitor interface statistics for signs of congestion or packet loss.

In addition to network-related issues, hardware or software problems can also contribute to poor VoIP call quality. Faulty network devices, outdated firmware, incompatible codecs, or misconfigured VoIP applications can all impact call quality and reliability. To address hardware or software issues, administrators should perform regular maintenance tasks such as firmware updates, software patches, and system diagnostics to ensure that VoIP infrastructure is functioning correctly. Additionally, conducting periodic VoIP system audits and performance tests can help identify potential issues before they impact call quality.

Furthermore, environmental factors such as network topology, network load, and network equipment configuration can also influence VoIP call quality. By conducting thorough network assessments and capacity planning exercises, administrators can identify potential bottlenecks, optimize network resources, and ensure adequate bandwidth availability for VoIP traffic. Additionally, implementing network redundancy and failover mechanisms can help minimize downtime and ensure continuous VoIP service availability in the event of network failures or outages.

Overall, troubleshooting VoIP call quality issues requires a comprehensive understanding of network protocols, voice codecs, and network infrastructure components. By employing a systematic troubleshooting approach that involves network monitoring, packet analysis, performance tuning, and hardware/software maintenance, administrators can effectively diagnose and resolve VoIP call quality problems, ensuring optimal voice communication experiences for users across the organization.

Addressing video conferencing performance problems is crucial for ensuring smooth and effective communication in today's digital workplace environment. Video conferencing has become an integral part of business operations, enabling remote collaboration, virtual meetings, and real-time interactions among team members, clients, and partners. However, various factors can impact the performance of video conferencing systems, leading to issues such as poor video quality, audio/video synchronization problems, jittery or frozen video streams, and dropped calls. To address these performance problems effectively, network administrators must adopt a proactive approach that involves identifying, troubleshooting, and resolving the underlying issues affecting video conferencing performance.

One common issue that can affect video conferencing performance is insufficient bandwidth, which can result in choppy video playback, audio dropouts, and overall degraded call quality. Insufficient bandwidth can occur due to network congestion, limited internet connectivity, or inadequate Quality of Service (QoS) prioritization for video traffic. To address bandwidth-related issues, administrators can use network monitoring tools to analyze network traffic patterns and identify bandwidth bottlenecks. Additionally, implementing QoS policies to prioritize video traffic over other types of data can help ensure adequate bandwidth allocation for video conferencing applications.

Another factor that can impact video conferencing performance is network latency, which refers to the delay experienced by data packets as they travel between endpoints. High latency can cause audio/video synchronization problems, delays in response times, and overall sluggish performance during video calls. To troubleshoot latency issues, administrators can use network diagnostic tools to measure round-trip times (RTT) between endpoints and identify areas of excessive delay. By optimizing network routing, minimizing packet loss, and prioritizing video traffic through QoS policies, administrators can reduce latency and improve video conferencing performance.

Jitter is another common issue that can degrade video conferencing performance, particularly over congested or unreliable network connections. Jitter refers to the variation in packet arrival times, resulting in uneven video playback and audio/video synchronization problems. To mitigate jitter, administrators can implement jitter buffer mechanisms on video conferencing endpoints or routers to smooth out variations in packet arrival times. Additionally, deploying jitter buffering algorithms and adjusting buffer sizes can help compensate for network jitter and ensure consistent video quality during conferences.

Packet loss is also a significant factor that can impact video conferencing performance, leading to visual artifacts, frozen video frames, and audio/video synchronization issues. Packet loss can occur due to network congestion, hardware failures, or network configuration errors. To diagnose packet loss issues, administrators can use packet capture and analysis tools to inspect packet headers and payloads, identify dropped packets, and determine the root cause of packet loss. Additionally, optimizing network routing, upgrading network hardware, and implementing error correction mechanisms can help reduce packet loss and improve video conferencing performance.

In addition to network-related issues, hardware or software problems can also contribute to poor video conferencing performance. Outdated firmware, incompatible codecs, insufficient system resources, or misconfigured video conferencing applications can all impact call quality and reliability. To address hardware or software issues, administrators should perform regular maintenance tasks such as firmware updates, software patches, and system diagnostics to ensure that video conferencing infrastructure is functioning correctly. Additionally, conducting periodic performance tests and system audits can help identify potential issues before they impact video conferencing performance.

Furthermore, environmental factors such as lighting conditions, camera placement, and room acoustics can also influence video conferencing performance. By optimizing camera settings, adjusting lighting levels, and minimizing background noise, administrators can enhance the visual and audio quality of video conferences. Additionally, providing user training and support to ensure that participants are familiar with video conferencing best practices can help improve overall performance and user satisfaction.

Overall, addressing video conferencing performance problems requires a comprehensive approach that involves network optimization, hardware/software maintenance, and user education. By identifying and resolving the underlying issues affecting video conferencing performance, administrators can ensure smooth and effective communication experiences for users across the organization, enhancing collaboration, productivity, and business success.

Chapter 10: Disaster Recovery and Business Continuity Planning for Networks

Disaster recovery planning is an essential aspect of any organization's IT strategy, aiming to mitigate the impact of unforeseen events such as natural disasters, cyber-attacks, hardware failures, or human errors. These events have the potential to disrupt business operations, compromise data integrity, and incur significant financial losses. Therefore, implementing robust disaster recovery plans is crucial for ensuring business continuity, minimizing downtime, and safeguarding critical assets. Disaster recovery planning encompasses various components, including risk assessment, business impact analysis, data backup and replication, contingency planning, and testing procedures.

The first step in disaster recovery planning is conducting a comprehensive risk assessment to identify potential threats and vulnerabilities that could impact business operations. This involves evaluating various scenarios, such as power outages, floods, earthquakes, or cyber-attacks, and assessing their likelihood and potential impact on organizational assets. By understanding the potential risks, organizations can prioritize their disaster recovery efforts and allocate resources accordingly.

Following the risk assessment, organizations should perform a business impact analysis (BIA) to determine the potential consequences of a disruptive event on critical business functions, processes, and systems. This involves identifying key dependencies, critical assets, and recovery time objectives (RTOs) for each business function. By quantifying the impact of downtime on revenue, customer satisfaction, and regulatory compliance, organizations can prioritize their recovery efforts and allocate resources effectively.

Once the risks and impacts have been identified, organizations can develop and implement a comprehensive disaster recovery plan that outlines procedures, responsibilities, and protocols for responding to and recovering from disruptive events. This plan should include detailed steps for data backup and replication, system recovery, infrastructure restoration, and communication protocols during emergencies. Additionally, organizations should establish clear escalation procedures, emergency contacts, and incident response teams to ensure a coordinated and effective response to disasters.

One of the fundamental components of disaster recovery planning is data backup and replication, which involves creating copies of critical data and storing them in secure locations to prevent data loss in the event of a disaster. Organizations can use various backup strategies, such as full backups, incremental backups, or differential backups, to ensure comprehensive data protection. Additionally, implementing data replication technologies, such as synchronous or asynchronous replication, can help ensure data availability and redundancy across multiple locations.

To deploy data backup and replication techniques effectively, organizations can leverage command-line interface (CLI) commands provided by backup and replication software solutions. For example, in a Linux environment, administrators can use the "rsync" command to synchronize files and directories between servers or storage devices. Similarly, in a Windows environment, administrators can use the "robocopy" command to perform file replication and synchronization tasks.

In addition to data backup and replication, organizations should also develop contingency plans for critical systems and applications to minimize downtime and maintain business continuity during disasters. This may involve implementing redundant hardware, failover mechanisms, or virtualization technologies to ensure rapid system recovery and service availability. By deploying redundant systems and failover mechanisms, organizations can minimize the impact of hardware failures or system outages on business operations.

Furthermore, disaster recovery plans should include regular testing and validation procedures to ensure their effectiveness and reliability. This involves conducting simulated disaster scenarios, tabletop exercises, or full-scale drills to assess the organization's readiness and response capabilities. By testing disaster recovery plans regularly, organizations can identify weaknesses, gaps, or bottlenecks in their recovery processes and make necessary improvements to enhance their resilience.

In summary, disaster recovery planning is essential for organizations to mitigate the impact of unforeseen events and ensure business continuity in the face of disasters. By conducting risk assessments, performing business impact analyses, implementing robust data backup and replication strategies, developing contingency plans, and testing recovery procedures regularly, organizations can minimize downtime, protect critical assets, and maintain customer trust and confidence even in the face of adversity.

Implementing business continuity measures for networks is crucial for ensuring uninterrupted operations and minimizing the impact of disruptive events on organizational productivity and profitability. Business continuity planning involves a proactive approach to identify potential risks, develop strategies to mitigate them, and establish procedures for maintaining essential functions during emergencies.

One of the primary steps in implementing business continuity measures for networks is conducting a comprehensive risk assessment to identify potential threats and vulnerabilities. This involves assessing various factors, such as natural disasters, cyber-attacks, equipment failures, or human errors, that could disrupt network operations. By understanding the potential risks, organizations can develop effective strategies to mitigate them and minimize their impact on business operations.

Once the risks have been identified, organizations can develop and implement a business continuity plan (BCP) that outlines procedures, responsibilities, and protocols for responding to and recovering from disruptive events. The BCP should include detailed steps for ensuring network availability, data protection, and system recovery during emergencies. Additionally, organizations should establish clear communication channels, emergency contacts, and incident response teams to facilitate a coordinated response to disasters.

Data backup and recovery are critical components of business continuity planning for networks. Organizations should implement robust backup strategies to ensure the integrity and availability of critical data in the event of a disaster. This involves regularly backing up essential data and storing copies in secure offsite locations to prevent data loss. Additionally, organizations should implement data replication technologies to ensure redundancy and failover capabilities for critical systems and applications.

To deploy data backup and recovery techniques effectively, organizations can leverage command-line interface (CLI) commands provided by backup and recovery software solutions. For example, administrators can use commands such as "rsync" in Linux environments or "robocopy" in Windows environments to synchronize files and directories between servers or storage devices. By automating backup tasks and scheduling regular backups, organizations can ensure the timely and reliable protection of critical data.

In addition to data backup and recovery, organizations should also implement measures to protect network infrastructure and ensure service availability during emergencies. This may involve deploying redundant network devices, such as routers, switches, and firewalls, to minimize single points of failure and enhance resilience. Additionally, organizations should implement failover mechanisms and load balancing techniques to ensure continuous service delivery and optimize network performance.

Another essential aspect of business continuity planning for networks is establishing communication and collaboration tools to facilitate remote work and enable seamless communication during emergencies. Organizations should deploy virtual private network (VPN) solutions, remote desktop services, and cloud-based collaboration platforms to ensure employees can access essential resources and communicate effectively from remote locations. By providing employees with the necessary tools and resources, organizations can maintain productivity and operational continuity during emergencies.

Furthermore, organizations should develop and conduct regular training and awareness programs to educate employees about business continuity procedures and their roles and responsibilities during emergencies. This may involve conducting tabletop exercises, simulation drills, or online training sessions to familiarize employees with emergency protocols and ensure they can respond effectively to various scenarios. By empowering employees with the knowledge and skills to handle emergencies, organizations can enhance their overall resilience and readiness to respond to disruptive events.

In summary, implementing business continuity measures for networks is essential for ensuring organizational resilience and maintaining operational continuity during emergencies. By conducting risk assessments, developing comprehensive business continuity plans, implementing robust data backup and recovery strategies, protecting network infrastructure, enabling remote work capabilities, and conducting regular training and awareness programs, organizations can minimize downtime, protect critical assets, and ensure the continuity of business operations even in the face of adversity.

Conclusion

In summary, the "Computer Networking Bootcamp: Routing, Switching, and Troubleshooting" bundle offers a comprehensive and structured approach to mastering the essentials of networking. Through four meticulously crafted books, readers are guided from foundational concepts in networking fundamentals to advanced routing protocols and troubleshooting mastery.

Book 1, "Networking Fundamentals: A Beginner's Guide to Routing Essentials," lays a solid groundwork by introducing readers to the fundamental principles of networking, including basic network concepts, protocols, and routing essentials. It provides beginners with a clear understanding of how networks function and sets the stage for more advanced topics covered in subsequent books.

Book 2, "Switching Strategies: Intermediate Techniques for Network Optimization," builds upon the foundational knowledge acquired in the first book by delving into intermediate-level switching techniques. Readers learn advanced switching concepts, such as VLANs, spanning tree protocols, and EtherChannel, to optimize network performance and scalability.

Book 3, "Advanced Routing Protocols: Mastering Complex Network Configurations," takes readers deeper into the intricacies of routing protocols, including OSPF, EIGRP, and BGP. It explores complex network configurations and teaches readers how to design, implement, and troubleshoot robust routing solutions for enterprise environments.

Book 4, "Troubleshooting Mastery: Expert Solutions for Resolving Network Challenges," equips readers with the skills and techniques needed to diagnose and resolve a wide range of network issues effectively. With real-world scenarios and practical troubleshooting strategies, readers learn how to identify problems, analyze symptoms, and implement solutions to keep networks running smoothly.

Together, these four books provide a comprehensive learning experience that empowers readers to become proficient in networking, routing, switching, and troubleshooting. Whether you are a novice seeking to enter the field of networking or an experienced professional looking to enhance your skills, the "Computer Networking Bootcamp" bundle offers invaluable insights and practical guidance to help you succeed in today's dynamic IT landscape.

www.ingramcontent.com/pod-product-compliance
Lightning Source LLC
Chambersburg PA
CBHW071234050326
40690CB00011B/2108